The
God of
Great
Surprises

The God of Great Surprises

D. James Kennedy

TYNDALE HOUSE PUBLISHERS
Wheaton, Illinois

Coverdale House Publishers Ltd.
London, England

Library of Congress Catalog Card Number 72-96220
ISBN 8423-1060-6, cloth; 8423-1061-4, paper

Copyright © 1973 by D. James Kennedy

Second printing, October 1973

Printed in the United States of America

Contents

I Promise You

When you and I come to the end of our lives and look back over the days God has given us, we will see that everything has been based upon the promises of God. If this is a new thought to you and if it can get hold of your mind now, your life could be revolutionized.

Everything that goes on in this world is the unfolding of the promises of God. You say, "There are a lot of things going on that just aren't pleasant — all sorts of terrible things." Yes, some of God's promises are just like that: certain consequences are promised for certain conditions. What you are seeing worked out in all of the problems and miseries is the fulfillment of the promises of God. He promised certain things would happen if certain things were done. He promised Adam and Eve they would die if they ate the forbidden fruit — they ate and they died. It was the fulfillment of God's promise.

For us who are Christians, the wonderful promises of God should be exceedingly precious. The Bible says that we are given extremely great and precious promises. These promises are blank checks, signed by God and given to us. To be used they must simply be claimed by faith.

Do you *believe* the promises of God? "Why, certainly I believe the promises of God!" But do you? Are you really claiming them? Are you cashing and spending them? We cannot truly believe God's promises unless we actually use them. Do you *pray* the promises of God? The only truly confident prayer is the one based on what God has actually promised.

Suppose someone wrote you a check for a million dollars, and assured you the check was good. You responded, "Sure, I believe it's a good check" — but, even though you were in desperate need, you just let it lie there on the dressing table, day after day, month after month, uncashed and unspent. I would have to conclude that you really didn't believe the check was good after all! I think this is the attitude many of us have about the promises of God. We consider them good enough to "believe in," but not good enough to actually put into practice. We forget that "what God has promised he is able also to perform."

Nature itself bears silent but eloquent witness to the truthfulness of God's promises. Thousands of years ago, shortly after the flood, God promised that springtime and harvest time would follow in their regular succession until the end of the world, that nothing would interrupt the regular progression of the seasons. And so Spring comes forth each year bearing in her arms the waking infant of nature . . . followed by Summer with flowers adorning her hair . . . then Fall with vines entwined on his legs and arms and the corn on his back . . . and finally, shaking with the frost, old man Winter. One after another they come. Each year they place one hand on the broad table of nature and raise the other hand to the sky and solemnly swear that the promises of God are true.

History, too, is one long unfolding of the promises of God, a proof that he is doing exactly what he said he would do. The whole history of the people of Israel is one huge picturebook lesson that even a child can read, illustrating dramatically the truthfulness of the promises of God. Yet so many of us stumble along as spiritual paupers when we could and should be spiritually rich, if only we would claim what God has promised. If we would spend every day of the coming month studying the promises of God, and then praying them and believing them, our whole lives would be changed. Our fears would be changed to courage, our timidity to confidence, our discouragement to radiant expectation for the future.

Have you received the promises of God? Let us start with the most important promise of all. God offers you eternal life. "He that believeth on me shall never perish." "What must I do to be saved?" cried the trembling Philippian jailer from his knees as he looked up into the face of the Apostle Paul. The answer came back as a promise from heaven: "Believe on the Lord Jesus Christ and thou shalt be saved, and thy house." Have you claimed that promise? Do you really believe these words? You may be saying, "That's too simple." The gospel is indeed simple — so simple that "the wayfaring man, though a fool, need not err therein." Anyone who takes Christ at his word receives eternal life.

If you have trusted in Jesus Christ for your salvation, if you have put your whole hope in the Cross of Christ and not in your own supposed merits which God regards as worthless for getting to heaven, if you have ceased to trust in your own works of self-righteousness and have put your trust in Christ, then you have his promise, "He that believeth on the Son shall never perish." It is undeserved, unmerited, unworked for, and paid for by Christ alone. Do you have eternal life? Are you going to heaven? If you say, "I don't know," you should question whether you actually believe God's promise. When we disbelieve God's promises we are in effect labeling him a liar (1 John 5:10).

But there is much more. Jesus promised that anyone who comes to him will be received. He promises us a loving welcome, a hearty reception. He says, "All that the Father giveth me shall come unto me, and him that cometh unto me I will in no wise cast out." You say, "I'm not fit to come to Christ. He won't receive me; I'm not good enough." You are absolutely right — you're not good enough! But that has nothing to do with whether or not he will receive you. We are accepted even though we are entirely and totally unacceptable. We are accepted for Christ's sake, not for our own sake. Christ specializes in receiving sinful men. "Him that cometh unto me I will in no wise cast out."

I don't care what you are . . . I don't care what kind of business dealings you have been engaged in . . . I don't care what kind of cheating you have been doing on your wife — or your husband — or in school . . . I don't care what kind of secret sin you are harboring . . . if you will come to Christ he will transform you and forgive you right where you are — right now. His promise is, "Him that cometh unto me I will in no wise cast out."

Perhaps you have received Christ. Perhaps you rejoiced in your salvation and things went well for a while. Then you fell into some serious sin and now you cannot even look up into his face. You hang your head. Your fellowship is broken. You are no longer aware of his presence. You feel dirty, unclean, unworthy. You cannot even go to him in prayer. What can you do? Martin Luther once felt that he virtually saw Satan standing in his room and saying to him, "Martin Luther, when you stand before the judgment, in that hour I will cause the whole world to know what you really are. I will cause everyone to know what your sins are and everything else about you." Luther responded, "Devil, you don't know the half of it. I'm actually twice as bad as you think, but when you finish telling what you know, then I have a word to add, and it is this: 'The blood of Jesus Christ, God's Son, cleanses me from all sin.' "

What sin have you committed that the Son of God cannot cleanse away? "I will wash you and make you whiter than snow . . . I will take your sins and place them as far from you as the east is from the west; I will bury them in the depths of the sea, never to remember them against you any more." God is willing to forget. His mercy is new each morning and fresh each day. Perhaps you are weary, tired of your failures. He says, "Come unto me, all ye that labor and are heavy laden, and I will give you rest." Come to him in prayer, come to him in his Word, come to him in meditation — and Christ will give you rest. "Take my yoke upon you, and learn of me; for I am meek and lowly in heart." If we could get away from our pride, our arrogance, our self-inflated ego, and instead see his lowliness, we would find rest for our souls.

Perhaps your need is that you are afraid of life . . . it is more than you can handle . . . it is too big for you . . . you don't know what to do with it . . . you can't really even do your job right . . .

you can't take care of your family . . . school is towering over you and threatens to crush you. Here is a promise right from the Word of God with your name on it: "I can do all things through Christ which strengtheneth me." Grasp hold of that with both hands and hold on! "I can do *all* things through Christ which strengtheneth me." This is not egoistic self-confidence but far nobler — *Christ*-confidence.

I myself have learned how to get hold of this verse. There was a time when I was afraid of my own shadow. I could no more have spoken to a crowd than I could have flown to the moon. But I took Christ at his word. I astonish even myself today at some of the things I take on — but the Lord brings me through them. I don't care what the challenge is because I believe that I can do all things through Christ which strengtheneth me. I'm not afraid of life anymore because he who has already won the victory dwells in my heart.

We have such wonderful promises of prayer. "Whatsoever ye ask in prayer, believing . . ." Believe that you have it and it is yours. He promises to hear and answer even before we ask. Are you concerned about your decisions of life? About what to do next? He says, "Lean not unto thine own understanding. In all thy ways acknowledge him, and he shall direct thy paths. . . . I will guide you with my eyes." He will make your life rich and fruitful. He says that we can be spiritually fruitful Christians, that he will fill us with his Spirit. He will cause us to bear much fruit: "He that abideth in me, and I in him, the same bringeth forth much fruit: for without me ye can do nothing." Oh, that we would learn to abide in his Word and to abide in him in prayer!

Are you afraid to travel? To get on a plane? Listen to this promise: "Behold, I am with thee and will keep thee in all places whithersoever thou goest." But you've got problems; you've got enemies. Claim this: "No weapon that is formed against thee shall prosper; and every tongue that shall rise against thee in judgment thou shalt condemn."

In addition, he has promised never to leave us or to forsake us. Even when we come to that last dark valley known as death his promise is, "Yea though I walk through the valley of the shadow of death, I will fear no evil: for thou art with me." Are you a Christian? If you have come to the place where you can say, "I know I can walk through the valley of the shadow of death and I will not fear," then you know that Christ is with you and in you.

Furthermore, he has promised that he will "work all things together for our good." Oh, if we would just claim that promise! That whatever comes to us comes through the filter of a Father's love, and that he will change it by the amazing miracle of his grace to our own good!

But he has promised to do even more than that! He says, "Call unto me, and I will shew thee great and mighty things that thou knowest not of." God is a God of the great surprise. He has promised to show us things that we have never even envisioned. "Eye hath not seen, nor ear heard, neither have entered into the heart of man, the things which God hath prepared for them that love him."

May God grant to you and to me an unshakable faith in his never-failing Word. May we open that leather-bound checkbook of God and cash the promises of him who has promised to "supply all of our needs out of his riches in glory," that we might live our lives not as spiritual paupers but as the sons and daughters of the King.

Love Now!

Jesus Christ was crucified between two thieves — in a sense, so are we. Daily the two thieves of "yesterday" and "tomorrow" rob us of our joy, our effectiveness, and our peace. How are things coming along with your crucifixion? Is the thief of yesterday tearing apart your life with the memories, the frustrations, the guilts of past days and hours? Or is the thief of tomorrow tearing your insides with the tortures of fear and anxiety? Anxiety, you know, does not empty tomorrow of its trials — but it empties today of its joy. Neither does anxiety empty tomorrow of its sorrows — instead, it empties today of its strength.

The Bible says, "Now there abideth faith, hope, and love, but the greatest of these is love." With these words we are brought face to face with the three great time elements in which we live. Faith looks back to the past, to take hold of the Cross of Jesus Christ, an historic event nailed down in time at the hill of Calvary. Faith takes hold of that Cross and claims the merits of Jesus Christ and captures the promises of God which say, "He that believeth on me shall never perish." Hope reaches out into the future and sees that life has a destination and eternal meaning. But faith and hope, both working together, focus our attention on the *present* in the realm of love. For love can only act in the present. You cannot love yesterday, and you cannot love tomorrow. You can only love now. "And there abideth faith, hope, and love, but the greatest of these is love. Make love your aim."

In this great procession of time we can never do anything at any other time than *now*. Author Keith Miller says that for too long he found he had lived in two unreal worlds: the unreal world of yesterday, and the unreal world of tomorrow. The world of yesterday cannot be changed, for "the hand writes, and having written moves on, and what is written cannot be changed." All of your sorrows and grief and tears will not wipe away the results of yesterday. The world of tomorrow, too, is an unreal world because it does not yet exist. It is still out there in the mists of the future. But for so many of us the ghosts of yesterdays past and tomorrows unborn torment our lives and rob us of all our joy and peace. But we can only live in the now. Running ceaselessly through the history of man is the *now, the golden now,* the *ever-present now*. There is indeed a tide in the affairs of men — it is the *now of today*.

Did you ever notice that some people seem to have a special sense of presence, of *living?* As the New World Singers said in one of their songs, "They're alive to their fingertips." They're brimming full. There's something exciting about these people — something different about them! They've impressed you. They've had an effect on your life. When you were with them, something happened — they seemed to bring you alive. They sort of live in the "Pepsi Generation." Do you know that kind of person? I believe that these are the people who have learned to live in the now.

Keith Miller describes this experience with an illustration which is very apt. He says that God has given us a heart and a mind, and that we are able with this heart and mind to focus our attention on certain things, objects, or people. In a very real sense this focusing of our attention with our whole heart is our true inner self. It is the focusing of all that we are upon a given situation. The Bible puts it this way: "Whatsoever thy hand findeth to do, do it with all thy might." Do it now. The beam of light which we focus on another person is the essence of what we really are.

Talking to some people is like talking to a lighthouse. The beam of their attention focuses on you briefly and then flashes away in wide circles. A little later it comes back and hits you again. "Hi! How are things in there?" But then the beam is gone again. Do you know that type of individual? They're looking to the past . . . then to the future. "Let me check my watch; I've got an appointment to keep . . . there's tomorrow . . . there's the burden of next month overwhelming me." They always seem to have at least one eye cocked on each of these things. I guess you would call this type of person a "practical half-wit." At least they never seem to bring all of their wits to bear upon the individual with whom they are talking.

Other people seem to be constantly unable to focus their mind. Their lives have a sort of dull glow that goes off in all directions at once but never focuses sharply anywhere. Miller shows us that down this blurred beam of our attention the love of Jesus Christ comes and focuses through our minds upon other human beings. This is perhaps the greatest way that we can love another person. We give them not just the labors of our hands but *ourselves* — what we really are inside; we empty this out and focus it upon them. This has fantastic power.

There spring to mind all sorts of incidents I have read in the histories of great men. These were seemingly insignificant events — events in which "little people" crossed the paths of these men of renown. Yet these men focused all of the attention of their hearts and their minds upon these seemingly insignificant persons; they loved them by pouring themselves out upon them, and changed their lives by that encounter. This is the secret that makes men great.

Years ago I studied speech and particularly reading. Do you know why some people can read aloud and capture your attention with the picture they paint? This is why: the reader focuses all his attention upon the very word that he is reading, not thinking three words ahead of himself and dissipating all of the emotional and intellectual impact of the words he is speaking.

Is this not true in sports? "Keep your eye on the ball," says the tennis pro. But I want to see where the opposition is, and so I line up my strategy — and I haul off and miss the ball altogether. "Keep your eye on the ball," says the golf pro . . . but I want to see where it's going! And so there goes my head and there goes the ball! Miller says that he came to see that in all of his life he was failing to take stock in the present moment. He was looking for a big "something" which was going to come tomorrow. Then he discovered that right here and now, each moment, was the only moment there was! And he could transform this into an important moment for God by loving other people right where he was.

He had been waiting for some big, important person to speak to for Christ and to impress for Christ and to win to Christ. He found that he was sort of marching into the future with his eyes focused on the horizon while there were countless numbers of what seemed to be little, unimportant people all around him passing by as one big blur. Then, as though his eyes had suddenly focused, he saw these people right here and now. He began to show his interest, to ask about them, to find out about their families and their concerns. He saw that they were real, live people. The love of God began to work through him until every day became an exciting adventure with Jesus Christ. He didn't have to wait for some big event in the future. Right now he could live and love for Christ.

This is a thrilling concept, isn't it? I wonder how many of you have found that your own lives have been robbed by the thieves of yesterday or tomorrow. I wonder how many people *you* are robbing this way. "Daddy, Daddy, look at me, Daddy! Look at this!" "Um-m-m? Oh yes, Honey, that's very interesting." "But Daddy!" "Yes, that's fine, Honey. Thank you . . ." And back to the paper again! Psychologists tell us that one of the worst things we can do to our children is to give them half of our interest, because to give them half of our interest is to give them half of ourselves. A half-wit is someone who is not all there. Let's not be half-wits with our children — let's be all there.

How about it, husband? How about it, wife? Are you a half-wit in your marriage? Are you giving your partner half attention instead of fullness of affection? Many a marriage has been ruined by this tragedy.

Recently a lady came to my counseling office and told me, "My husband's never there. Two-thirds of him is left at the office." How many a mate has gone to his or her beloved and tried to express love, but the other partner just wasn't all there. He was living in the past — hostilities, animosities, frustrations, fears, failures. Or he was living in the future — what must be done the next hour, the next day, the next week. And so he just wasn't there when he was needed. He may have been there in body, but the beam of his heart and mind and love was not focused.

The Bible has a lot to say about now. It says that there is a God who is the same yesterday, today, and forever. He has existed forever and will exist forever and knows the end from the beginning. He knows all things. He has an infinite option of matters upon which to place his thoughts, but the amazing thing about God is that when we go to him in prayer he is *all there with us*. He understands thoroughly. Do you know what understanding means? It means that he looks sympathetically, empathetically, into our problems. God says that he is focusing the beam of his love upon us, a beam that flows from a Cross, a beam that has followed us all our lives and which we have ignored. God asks us to focus our attention, for there is life for a look at the crucified One. This is trust — turning our hopes, our hearts, our minds to the Cross. This is faith — receiving him into our hearts with joy, for this is what he wants us to do. He wants to shine the beam of his love into our lives and transform our hearts.

"Now is the accepted time . . . now is the day of salvation." The Bible says we need take no anxious thought for the morrow. But the only way we can do this is if God has become our Father . . . if we have been adopted into the family of God by faith in Jesus Christ; then he promises that he will provide all of our needs. "Your Father knoweth what things ye have need of. . . . Therefore, take no thought for the morrow."

There is a second stipulation: "Seek first the kingdom of God and his righteousness, and all of these things shall be added unto you . . . Therefore take no thought for the morrow. . . . Sufficient unto the day is the evil thereof." Don't haul all of tomorrow's anxieties and worries into today. As someone said, "Today —

this bright and beautiful God-filled day — is the tomorrow that once you so dreaded. For tomorrow's cares will bring with them tomorrow's God."

Have you come to the day of salvation? If you cannot say, "I have received the love of Christ; I have received Christ as my Savior and Lord; I have accepted the gift of eternal life; I have been adopted into the family of a Father who is providing all of my needs and is expending much care for me in heaven;" then the words "Be not anxious for tomorrow" are not for you. Only those who have responded to the love of Christ and have this love in their hearts can do what we are talking about here. Only those who have a faith anchored to Calvary and a hope anchored to eternity can live a life of love without guilt, a life without anxiety or worry in the *now*. Where do you live?

To Tell the Truth

Some children in Sunday school had been learning Bible verses — but sometimes they got them confused. The quiz question was "What is the definition of a lie?" Johnny popped smartly to his feet and replied, "A lie is an abomination unto the Lord and a very present help in time of trouble!"

Do you believe in telling the truth? Or do you believe that sometimes it is necessary to tell a lie? Surveys show that at least 60 percent of the American people feel that occasionally it is necessary to twist the truth.

Is this what you believe? If so, religion is on your side! Mohammed wrote in the *Koran* that there are two times when it is justifiable to tell a lie without sinning. (Interestingly, both of these situations are restricted to women). A woman may tell a lie, Mohammed wrote, in order to save a life or during times of war. Speaking for the Hindu religion, Krishna wrote in the Mahabharata that there are five kinds of lies which are sinless: lies in connection with marriage, lies for the gratification of lust, lies to save one's life, lies to protect one's property, and lies in behalf of a Brahman (Hindu holy man). If you believe it is necessary to lie at times, the pagan religions are on your side!

However, God is diametrically opposed to such things. The Bible and the Christian faith teach clearly that there is no circumstance, no condition, in which it is ever justifiable to tell a lie.

What does the Word of God specifically say about the issue of truth and falsehood? In this day when society is being torn apart by countless lies, when there is a credibility gap between the White House and the people, between one nation and another, between husband and wife, between generation and generation, it seems to me that once more we need to hear what the Word of God has to say about this subject.

The God of all truth says, "All his ways are judgment: a God of truth without iniquity . . . Thou hast redeemed me, O Lord God of truth . . . For the word of the Lord is right; and all his works are done in truth . . . I have not concealed thy lovingkindness and thy truth from the great congregation . . . Behold, thou desirest truth in the inward parts . . . Mercy and truth are met together; righteousness and peace have kissed each other . . . He shall judge the world with righteousness, and the people with his truth . . . The lip of truth shall be established for ever, but a lying tongue is but for a moment . . . He that doeth the truth is loved by the Lord: O Lord, art not thine eyes upon the truth . . . And the Word was made flesh and dwelt among us (and we beheld his glory, the glory as of the only begotten of the Father) full of grace and truth . . . Then said Jesus, I am the way, the truth, and the life . . . The Spirit of truth . . . Howbeit when he, the Spirit of the truth, is come, he will guide you into all truth . . . Sanctify them through thy truth: thy word is truth . . . Pilate saith unto him, What is truth? . . . But we are sure that the judgment of God is according to truth against them which commit such things."

Consider these words of Scripture too.

"Thou shalt not bear false witness . . . Ye shall not steal, neither deal falsely, neither lie one to another. Ye shall not swear by my name falsely . . . Ye are forgers of lies, ye are all physicians of no value . . . My lips shall not speak wickedness, nor my tongue utter deceit . . . Thou shalt destroy them that speak falsehoods; the Lord will abhor the bloody and deceitful man . . . Keep thy tongue from evil, and thy lips from speaking guile . . . Thou lovest evil more than good, and lying rather than to speak righteousness . . . God shall likewise destroy thee for ever . . . The words of his mouth were smoother than butter, but war was in his heart; his words were softer than oil, yet were they drawn swords . . . But thou, O God, shall bring them down into the pit of destruction; bloody and deceitful men shall not live out half their days; . . . The wicked are estranged from the womb: they go astray as soon as they be born, speaking lies . . . They delight in lies: they bless with their mouth, and they curse inwardly . . . He that worketh deceit shall not dwell within my house . . . I hate and abhor lying . . . These six things doth the Lord hate: yea, seven are an abomination unto him: a proud look, a lying tongue, etc. . . . Lying lips are an abomination to the Lord . . . The getting of treasures by a lying tongue is a vanity tossed to and fro of them that seek death . . . Ye are of your father the devil, and the lusts of your father ye will do. He was a murderer from the beginning, and abode not in the truth, because there is no truth in him. When he speaketh a lie, he speaketh of his own: for he is a liar, and the father of it . . . Because I tell you the truth, ye believe me not . . . Putting away lying, speak every man truth with his neighbor . . . All liars shall have their part in the lake which burneth with fire and brimstone . . . And there shall in no wise enter into it (the Holy City) anything that . . . maketh a lie."

Do you believe in telling lies? The Bible makes it very plain that God is a God of truth. The triune God — Father, Son, and Holy Spirit — is at the very core of his being the God of truth. All of his works are truth; all of his words are truth. It is impossible that God should lie. The very essence of deity is truth itself. It is equally true that the very essence of character is this same pure truth. All of the virtues of man can be summarized in one all-important word — *truth*.

All other virtues are simply truth in deed or truth in action. The man that will lie on one occasion will lie on another. The man that will lie in word will lie in deed. Impurity is nothing more than falsehood in action. Truth is the foundation of all genuine character. When you examine the character of a man you are really asking, "Is he truthful? Is he true to his word? Is he true to what he says he believes? Is he true to what he professes to be doing? Or is he a deceitful man, a hypocrite, a living lie?"

Absolute veracity is what is required by God in his Word. Nothing less will suffice. There is no place under any circumstance, under any condition, when any sort of lie may be justified, according to the teaching of the Word of God. Without getting overly technical, a lie is defined as telling a falsehood with the intention to deceive (which distinguishes it from a mistake, where there is no intention to deceive).

Ingenious people have devised various exceptions to the rule of truth. Jeremy Taylor wrote a book in which he said there were three exceptions. He said it was all right to lie to the insane, to children, and to criminals: to the insane, because they were incapable of judging truth or falsehood; to children, if our lies were benevolently inclined; and to criminals, if we could by this means prevent further acts of crime.

In contrast, the head of one mental institution reports that the basis for all progress with the insane is that they be told nothing but the truth at all times. Only by this means can there be any hope that these sufferers will be delivered from the world of falsehood and unreality in which they continually live.

If there is any group of people that deserve and need to hear the truth it is children. A boy came to his teacher crying bitterly over his sin of exaggeration. He said it was his great problem — but also his mother's. Lying parents produce lying children. God holds parents responsible for the deceit they practice in the presence of their children.

How about lying to criminals? We may avoid losing our money in the safe if we say we don't know the combination! Someone asked D. L. Moody what he would do in this situation. He replied, rather tersely, that he wouldn't be in that situation! If we walk with God we will indeed avoid many awkward situations. The little boy said that a lie was a very present help in trouble, but the Bible says that *the Lord* is a very present help in trouble. Why should we turn to lies to help us when the God of the universe has sworn that he will never forsake us?

Some people argue that lying can be justified if the motive is right and the goal is noble. To lie for raw self-interest is very wrong, they say, but to lie in order to help another person is permissible or even desirable, in some cases. But what does the Bible say about this kind of reasoning? In Romans, chapter three, the Apostle Paul has something to say to people who assert that the end justifies the means — that it is all right to do evil if the goal is good. Here is what the Apostle says: "Their damnation is just!" (Romans 3:8).

Professional medical people are often quoted in order to prove that telling a lie is acceptable if the motive is right. But listen to this doctor: "When I graduated from medical school I took the advice of my colleagues and practiced lying for five years. I was told that if I thought it would be better for my patients that I avoid telling them the truth, then I would lie to them and to their friends and to anyone else I thought necessary. After five years I realized the fallacy of this course of action and I reversed this practice completely. I began to tell the truth or tell nothing at all. For fifteen years I have followed this principle and find it to be infinitely better. I find that people usually want to know the truth about themselves, and that even when they are dying they have the strength and courage to face this fact."

I would like to speak personally to each of you who has a relative or loved one with a terminal disease. Have you lied to this loved one? Have you promised him or her life when you knew his fate was death? I can speak personally here because I have faced this situation in my own family. At issue here is a whole view of life, a whole standard of values. *It is a false view of life* to believe that our temporary physical lives are so important that we can sacrifice integrity, honor, virtue, and truth itself in order to gain a few more hours of false tranquillity.

Is there hope for us? Can we lie against society, against Christ, against truth itself and still hope to find forgiveness from God? I ask you to look at Truth personified — the Lord Jesus Christ.

When Truth came down to this earth, liars fell upon him and nailed him to a Cross. There on that Cross he took upon himself our lies and our sins, and endured their just penalty in our place.

Having died in our stead, he offers to freely give us eternal life, forgiveness, pardon, and cleansing from sin if we will genuinely receive him into our heart. And then we have the true Word of God, which tells us that whoever trusts in God's Son shall never perish: ". . . he shall not come into condemnation, but is passed from death unto life."

I invite you to accept his promise, "He that has the Son has life, and he that believeth not this record which God has given of his Son has made God a liar."

They Did Me Wrong!

The way a person reacts to people who wrong him is perhaps the truest revelation of his real character. Nothing draws the line more quickly between a genuine Christian and a non-Christian than the way he reacts to those who hurt him. We're talking about what happens in your heart and mine when someone says something that cuts us to the quick . . . when someone treats us unfairly . . . when our wife lets us have it again . . . when our husband forgets our anniversary again. When these things happen to us, how do we react? I believe there are basically only four ways that we react to such mistreatment. Let's look at these responses.

The first reaction is one of anger. This is the law of the jungle. If you make a tiger angry you need not wonder what the end result will be! Similarly, the reaction of human anger is the unbridled and untamed unleashing of the fury of man against his fellow man. Here we are seen in our closest relationship to the beast. It means that when someone does me dirt, I'm going to get him! I'm going to get him when I can and in the best way I can, so long as I don't hurt myself more in doing so. In fact, I would probably bash his brains out except that I'd end up in prison!

God didn't create us this way. God made man in a paradise.

He made him perfect, so that his heart knew nothing but love. But man sinned and rebelled against God. He refused to have God rule over him. The Bible says that man plunged instantly into sin, and death crept over the human soul. Though physically alive, he became spiritually dead. The reaction is seen in the very next generation, as Abel causes his brother Cain to be jealous, and just this little jealousy causes Cain to react with violent anger. He bides his time, waiting until Abel is out in the field, his back turned. Then Cain picks up a stone and smashes his brother's skull and says, in effect, "That's what you get for doing me dirt!" Fortunately, most people who react that way today are in prison.

But there is another reaction we can demonstrate. It is the reaction of justice. By the influence of the Holy Spirit, man has been slowly carried up out of the barbarism of his past and into the civilization of the Christian era. This, of course, was the purpose of the famous commandment of the Old Testament, "An eye for an eye and a tooth for a tooth." People sometimes react to this commandment in horror. "Oh, my! What a horrible doctrine! How could the Bible teach such a thing!" They are simply saying that they are ignorant of what the Bible teaches and why it teaches it. We must realize that the context of the giving of this teaching was not the context of the love of Christ but the atmosphere of a barbarous civilization. "An eye for an eye and a tooth for a tooth" was meant to teach people not to take a *head* for an eye and a *life* for a tooth, which was the common practice of the day. The punishment was to be restricted to fit the crime. This is the reaction of justice.

This is truly a long step up from wrath; yet it is insufficient. Nevertheless, it is a principle which many people use: "It's only fair . . . He should get what's coming to him . . . if somebody hits you, hit him back . . . don't let them run all over you! . . . stand up for your rights . . . justice!" But how far this is from the teachings of Christ! Though there is nothing wrong with justice, there is something far higher.

Before we consider this higher principle, I think we ought to look carefully at a third reaction we sometimes have. This reaction is very common in a civilized society, especially in a Christian society, where the teachings of Christ against retaliating, against striking back, are well known. People often use this reaction to avoid being completely barbaric — they think! — not realizing how far they have fallen short of what Christ has taught us. This is what we might call the reaction of avoidance. It goes something like this: "Oh, no. I'm not going to do anything to him. I won't retaliate. No, I forgive him. I just don't want to have anything to do with him! Don't expect me to go where he is. We're through!" Is this forgiveness? I suggest that such a person doesn't know what the word forgiveness means!

Does God forgive us like that? Does God say, "Oh yes, you're forgiven. Forget it. I'll never think another thought about it. It's all over. But it's also all over between you and me. I won't have anything more to do with you. Never again. Stay away." Thank God, he doesn't deal with us like that! Rather, the forgiveness of God reaches out with its infinite grace and draws us back to his heart with the tenderest and strongest bond. Christian forgiveness will likewise inevitably result in reconciliation — not avoidance. If there is someone you say you have forgiven, but whom you intend always to avoid, God says you have no more forgiven that person than the man who strikes out against him. You have only covered up your lack of forgiveness by concealing it in your heart, not realizing that it still lurks there as a poison, destroying your soul.

Of course, this approach to our persecutors is a little awkward for those of us who have to live in the same house with the person who has hurt us. This complicates the situation and frequently causes us to employ "Variation A" of the avoidance approach: just pretend the other person doesn't exist — as much as that is possible! This is what we call the "deep freeze." It's a cold shoulder that extends all the way to the little toe. Have you ever experienced that? It hangs like ice in the house, and the silence crunches beneath the foot like dry snow on a cold night! If by chance one of those awful situations should arise in which someone is forced to speak, it is very evident from the chilly tone of the voice that the thermostat has been turned down below freezing and that the inside walls of the heart are very much in need of defrosting. Have you ever experienced this?

Then there is the look. Do you know this look? It's that chilling look in which icicles protrude from the eyes, piercing and freezing your soul. The real tragedy of "the look" is that those who use it think they have forgiven because they have not burst out in hot retaliation.

Anger . . . justice . . . avoidance. . . . Each of these reactions to injury of spirit lacks a crucial ingredient: Christian love.

Christ taught us to love our enemies. This is perhaps the most characteristic sign of a Christian: "By this shall all men know that ye are my disciples, because ye love one another." Nothing reveals a higher form of love than to love our enemies. Here the natural man (the unregenerate man, the man whose heart has never been transformed by Christ living in his soul) finds that this is something that is hopelessly beyond him. He may remain civil, but in his heart he still remains hostile. He cannot free himself from this hostility. Only Jesus Christ can do this. It was Christ who turned the whole ancient world upside down by replacing the mailed fist with the pierced hand. This revolutionary ethic was not only taught by Christ, but lived by him. It can be triumphantly relived by each of us who has Christ in his heart.

One of my favorite stories concerns a young married woman who had a problem with her father-in-law. It was all his fault, you see, because he was an old grouch; furthermore, he had the gout, which made him even grouchier! He used to sit around with his foot wrapped, resting it on the kitchen stove. He would complain about what his daughter-in-law did and how she fixed the food, until she would get so mad she just couldn't stand it. She was a new Christian, having recently accepted Christ as her Savior; yet she was a high-spirited woman and would lose her temper and explode all over this man. Then there would be long, frosty days, until finally they would become civil again. Finally she went to her minister and told him the whole story. "I just can't control myself," she said. "What can I do?" "What does he like to eat most?" asked the minister. She said, "Fudge." "Next time he does this make him some fudge," responded the minister. She went home thinking that he was evidently an immature minister, and perhaps the congregation should consider looking around for someone with more experience. . . .

A few days later she was in the kitchen fixing dinner. Her father-in-law was there, too, resting his foot on the stove. She tripped and spilled hot water on his foot. And there it came! — that flow of foul language that poured so naturally from his mouth. He cursed her and told her what he thought of her again. As she stood there she felt her body turning red all the way up to her ears. She was just about to explode all over him when she remembered the advice of the preacher. She said a little prayer, turned away, went over to the refrigerator, and began to prepare the fudge! She got out the milk, the chocolate, and all the other ingredients and began to whip up her fudge. By the time it was ready for the stove Dad had folded his arms and gone back to sleep. After the fudge was cooked she put it in the refrigerator to cool. When it was done she sliced it and put it on a plate. Then she went over and placed it under his nose. He opened his eyes and looked down at the fudge. He just stared. He couldn't believe it! Finally, as a tear fell on the plate, he took down his foot and got off his chair and onto his knees. He put his arms around her waist and said, "Daughter, forgive a grouchy old man." And she had the joy of leading him to Christ right there in her kitchen.

"Be not overcome of evil, but overcome evil with good" (Rom. 12:21). The Reverend T. Stuart Holden was in Egypt with the Highland regiment. In the regiment was a large, burly sergeant who had recently been converted to Christ. Holden asked him how he had been converted. The sergeant replied, "When we were in Malta there was a private who became a Christian. We gave him an awful time. We mocked him and laughed at him. But he continued to read the Bible and to pray and to live a Christian life. It made me angry. The better the life he lived, the angrier I became. One day after this private had been on sentry duty he came in wet and tired. He prepared himself for bed and then got down on his knees, as was his custom, and began to pray. Just his attitude there on his knees in prayer made me furious. I was sitting next to him and had just taken off my boots. I took those boots and clobbered him on the side of the head! He reeled under the blow but continued to pray. I went to bed, my heart still filled with bitterness. When I awoke the next morning, to my utter amazement there beside my bed, beautifully polished, were those same boots! I couldn't believe it! This was his answer to my blow! My heart was melted, and I asked the One who could put such love into a human heart to come and dwell in my heart. And he did."

Did you ever hear of poetic justice? This is a situation in which somebody, perhaps a despotic king, has been accustomed to cutting peoples' heads off, but now his own head is coming off! We say, "That's poetic justice." But did you ever consider poetic love? Not words from a poet, but acts of love. Did you notice it in the incident of the boots, and of the fudge? He reviled her for her cooking, and she fixed him what he liked; he beat him with his boots, and so he polished them.

Jesus said, "Bless them that curse you; do good unto them that hate you. Pray for them which despitefully use you. . . ." When people speak evil of us and spread rumors, do we determine to become a rumormonger ourselves? Let us do it, and let us spread the best rumors we can about them! Matching the law to the sin — isn't this what Jesus did? He was condemned to the Cross, but in the midst of his condemnation he offered forgiveness to those who condemned him. This is what he calls us to do. Only at the Cross can we find power for this kind of love.

Sir Walter Scott was bothered once by a stray dog. Picking up a stone, he threw it at the dog, intending to frighten him away. But he had thrown it harder and straighter than he planned, and it hit the dog in the leg, breaking it badly. Instead of becoming vicious or running away, the dog limped up to him and licked his hand. Sir Walter Scott never forgot that. We, too, have thrown stones at God. Every sin, every act of rebellion is a stone cast at him. But Christ comes not with thunderbolts but with arms outstretched upon a Cross. There in the love of that Cross men find the power to forgive their enemies and to love them truly.

I've asked you how you treat people who have wronged you. Now I want to ask you how you will respond to the One who dearly loves you even though you have repeatedly wronged him — the Lord Jesus Christ. He died for you, and offers you eternal life freely. How will you react to this love? Will you spite Christ doubly by rejecting this overwhelming offer of his grace? Or will you respond to the love of Christ by freely receiving him into your heart?

He waits for your answer.

Words That Kill Marriages

If you were to sit with me behind the counseling desk in my office year after year and listen to the host of problems brought before me, I think you would agree that the most common problem that afflicts men and women is the problem of the marriage relationship. It is therefore only proper that we consider what the Bible has to say about this oldest of institutions, about this foundation of our society, about this bond which holds together church and state, but is being ripped apart in its very warp and woof today.

In any discussion on the problems of marriage, the first question we must ask is, "Where do we begin?" As I thought about this I considered some of the great problems that exist in marriage. I wrestled in my own mind for a starting point — then came up with one I had not expected. I am starting at a place which I feel is very basic because it is unsuspected. It goes unnoticed and unheralded, never makes the newspapers, very seldom comes out in the divorce courts, and yet is probably one of the greatest causes of failure in marriage. By failures in marriage I mean not only marriages that end up on the rocks of divorce, or even those that come to counselors' desks. I'm talking about the vast number of marriages that fail to come anywhere close to what God would like them to be.

Is your marriage what you hoped it would be? Some years ago

a man got his picture in newspapers from coast to coast because he did a most remarkable thing. He walked every step of the way from New York to California! At the end of his trek reporters asked him about his journey. They asked him if he ever thought he wouldn't make it. "Many times," he replied. They asked him what almost defeated him. He answered, "Let me tell you. It wasn't the rushing traffic in the cities or the blaring horns and screeching brakes of cabs or trucks. It wasn't even those interminable midwestern plains that just went on and on as if they would never end. Nor was it the ice-tipped mountains of the Rockies. It wasn't even the blazing sun over the desert. What almost defeated me over and over again was the sand in my shoes."

I believe this is true in most marriages. It is this unheralded, seldom-discussed sand in the shoes that defeats most people. In many cases it lies in the background of much more flagrant sins that make the papers and are written up in the divorce decrees. I'm thinking of the abrasive sand of criticism.

Let us consider this from several viewpoints. Let us look at it first in the relationship of the parent and child, for the relationship of child to parent eventually becomes that of mate to mate in adult life. Problems which are created and molded in childhood are later intensified in marriage.

A little baby is born. It kicks its feet and waves its arms and cries for attention. Soon it learns to talk. Some of the most frequently heard and repeated words are these: "Mommie, look! Mommie, look! Look, Daddy! It's a rabbit! I drew it myself! How do you like it, Daddy?" This first infantile verbalization expresses one of the most deep-seated needs of the human heart: acceptance and recognition from other human beings. Whether it is a baby holding up a picture of a bunny rabbit, or Napoleon marching on Moscow, it is really an expression of the same basic human need. Whether it is a baby crying, "Look, Mommie!" or a college student laboring for his A's, it is the same basic motivation — the quest for recognition, the search for acceptance by others.

I can hear the parents now with their sad, depressing tale. A seventeen- or eighteen-year-old boy stands in the living room and says, "Mom, Dad, I hate your guts! I never want to see you again!" And he doesn't! Crushed, the parents ask themselves, "What happened? What did we do? Where did we go wrong? We tried so hard to give him the best of everything — the best clothes, the best toys, the best school, the best food, the best doctors. Where did we go wrong?" Isn't this a pathetic cry? Where did they go wrong? It was the sand in the shoes. The kid just got sick of it.

A psychologist writing recently in a popular magazine described the difference between the way we treat guests in our home and the way we treat our children. Though we talk about these children as being little gifts from God, visitors from heaven in our household for just a little while, somehow we don't seem to treat them like that, do we? For example, what happens when a visitor comes to our house and spills the coffee on the floor? "Oh, that's all right! Don't think a thing of it!" and we wipe it up. "That's nothing! It's just a little old rug . . . coffee doesn't stain! It can happen to anybody. I do it all the time myself!"

But what happens when little Johnnie toddles out of the kitchen and — whoops! . . . there it goes! What invariably happens? He gets a three-part discourse. Like all Gaul, he is divided into three parts. The first part has to do with his past, the second with his character, and the third with his future prospects. It goes something like this: "Every time you do the same thing! You can never pick up anything without dropping it! You clumsy idiot! Can't you do anything right? How many times do I have to tell you? Don't you have any sense at all?" And on it goes.

Or the visitor comes in and says, "That's a lovely little vase you . . . Oops, I broke it!" "Oh, it's nothing at all!" (You got it in Istanbul, of course, but . . .) "I know just where to get another one." (You'll never get back there again but you would know just where to get one if you ever should!) But now Johnnie, or Mary, or Sue. If one of them should in his curiosity pick up the little vase and drop it, then you begin. The cork flies off, the steam rushes out, and the three parts begin — seasoned with gall. "You clumsy numbskull! How many times must I tell you! Every time you touch anything you break it! Can't you do anything right? Don't you have any sense at all? You'll never be able to get through school if you can't learn to do things better than that! You'll never be able to hold a job!"

"Mommie, Daddy . . . I hate your guts!" What did they do? Where did they go wrong? They went wrong because they failed to grasp one of the deepest needs of the human heart. What a sad thing to hear the words of a young man who had just murdered his father: "All I ever wanted you to do was recognize that I was here."

So the child grows up and gets married. He hopes that in marriage this deep, unconscious, often unexpressed need will be met. The girl likewise puts her whole hope of future happiness into the hands of her husband. And a big part of this is the need to be loved, the need to be accepted, the need to be appreciated. They hope that even if they didn't get this at home they will get it in their marriage.

But little by little disintegration begins. How foolish is the man or woman who thinks that a marriage license is a hunting license for faults! This is one of Satan's most brilliant devices, through which he has brought misery into countless homes. How foolish is the man or woman who falls into this deceitful trap! "Judge not, that ye be not judged . . . with what measure ye mete, it shall be measured unto you again."

Yes, ladies, you can get your husband to wipe his feet when he comes in the door. "There are those black marks again! I spent all day cleaning this room! Can't you ever remember to wipe your feet?" You can finally housebreak him that way and you will think you have gotten your point across. And you will have succeeded. But you will not realize that in seventeen other ways you will receive your measure again. You won't even know why or where it is coming from. One day you will say, "How could he have done that to me! What did I do? Where did I go wrong? How could he even have looked at her? I've been such a faithful wife." You've been faithful, all right — you have faithfully pointed out every fault in the man for twenty-five years! He's had enough sand in his shoes. "What can he possibly see in her? She's older than I am and uglier too!" But do you know something? She's probably a little smarter too because, amazingly, she can't even seem to see all of his faults! You wouldn't believe this, but she actually thinks there are some really nice things about him! And you know what? She tells him frequently.

But what we really need is not merely *avoiding criticism* but *looking for good*. The Bible puts it this way: "If there be any virtue, if there be any praise, think on these things."

Does this typify your relationship to your wife or to your husband? Are you a finder of *good* or a finder of *faults?* The tragedy of criticism is that the human spirit suffers the ultimate calamity: the very milk of human kindness curdles and the bloom of love just withers up and blows away. The whole atmosphere of the home becomes poisoned. People become afraid to say anything different or do anything different because of that criticism which lies just beneath the surface, ready to lash out and cut them down. Marriage partners find that they can no longer express love for their mate because of the rejection inherent in criticism. Love has withered in the atmosphere of rejection.

Oh, what our homes could be like if there were acceptance — if there were *good* finding and not *fault* finding! As a happy mate once said, "Thou hast reached out into my life and found those things that are good which no one else has been able to see." How often, instead, husbands and wives reach down into the lives of their spouses and find the bad things that no one else ever sees!

You don't treat anyone else this way. You don't carp at your friends. Yet you make the greater mistake of derogating the one on whom most of your hopes of happiness in this life depend. And you reap the harvest of misery.

Judging and criticizing are not just a problem — they are also a *sin*. "Judge not, that ye be not judged." It is disobedience to the command of God. How few people realize that in the very act of faultfinding they usually are more sinful than the person they are criticizing! They are probably doing infinitely more damage to their marriage than the fault that is being discussed!

The ironic foolishness of faultfinding is that it never does anything really constructive. It is always *destructive;* it recoils and strikes you in the back when you aren't looking. It is sin because it is trying to play God. "Who art thou, O man, that judgest another; wherein thou judgest another thou condemnest thyself. . . ." The next time you open your lips to find fault with another person, remember that you are condemning yourself. It is sin because it is an unwholesome attitude. It is the attitude of pride, the base heart attitude from which judgment proceeds. It is the proud person who finds fault with others.

Consider the Pharisee and the publican in the temple. The Pharisee said, "I thank thee, Lord, that I am not as other men." What an implicit criticism of the whole human race! "I don't do this; I don't do that. I'm not like that publican over there at the other end of the temple." But the publican would not so much as lift up his eyes to heaven, but smote his breast and cried, "O God, have mercy unto me, a sinner." No, the publican wasn't looking around finding fault with other people, because he had the spirit of contriteness; he had the spirit of humility, and all he could see was his own sin. This is what Jesus meant when he said that if you find a splinter in someone else's eye you've got a beam in your own eye. This is what the Scripture means when it says, *"Out of thy blindness and impenitent heart."* If that beam were taken out of our eye we would see this unhealthy attitude of pride disappear, because the light of God would flow into our souls and show us the vast abyss of sin that is in our own hearts. We would be humbled by our own condition and would have little time left to criticize others.

May I point out also that pride is a denial of the very principle of grace. God talks about this in the second chapter of Romans: "After thy hardness and impenitent heart treasurest up unto thyself wrath against the day of wrath and revelation of the righteous judgment of God." We *talk* about grace but we go out and behave contrary to it. Christ, however, did not so act. Jesus said, "I come not to condemn you but that the world might be saved." Jesus came with no judgmental attitude. To the woman taken in the very act of adultery he said, *"Woman, neither do*

I condemn thee; go thy way."

But may we never find fault with anyone? We may, but only if we do it in a biblical way. "Judge not" is in the present tense. It means "do not continually be judging other people." There may be occasions when we are required to judge. But the Bible spells out how. In Galatians 6:1 we read, "Brethren, if a man be overtaken in a fault, ye which are spiritual restore such an one in the spirit of meekness, considering thyself, lest thou also be tempted. Bear ye one another's burdens." "If a brother is overtaken with a fault" denotes not every little human imperfection but rather a more serious sin, something which ordinarily happens very seldom. "You that are spiritual. . . ." If we would consider this and bring ourselves up short, remembering our own nature and our own relationship to God, we would walk in the spirit of humility and prayer. "Consider thyself, lest thou also be tempted." And then bear one another's burdens.

This is what Jesus did. Instead of pointing out our faults to us, he took them upon himself as he bore on the Cross the burden of our guilt and the penalty of our sins. Jesus Christ accepts us as righteous. This is justification. This is the very essence of Christianity — that though we are sinners, we are accepted as though we were righteous! It is this attitude of acceptance which completely transforms men. It is the Christ who is the *friend* of sinners and not the *faultfinder* of sinners that changes the hearts of men.

In this fellowship love blossoms and a communion develops between our souls and Christ which even eternity will never dissolve. Oh, that God would show us his great principle of grace, the very genius of the Christian faith! Oh, that we might learn that love covers a multitude of sins, even as our sins have been covered by the love of Christ! Oh, that God would help us to accept every person for Christ's sake! Then we would find a new fellowship and communion blossoming in our homes; a new and deeper oneness in Christ. We would find that our reserve, our fear of rejection and condemnation, would dissolve and disappear in the presence of the overwhelming love of the Holy Spirit. This is God's will for each of us.

Rebellion Begins at Home

Little Susan was four years old. She had attended Sunday school almost since birth. She knew a number of verses by now and had learned to say her prayers at mealtime and at other times. But today she had been naughty and was being punished. Her dinner was being served on a TV tray placed neatly in the corner of the room, with Susan facing the corner all by herself. Of course this tugged at the parents' hearts, so they listened with eager ears as she bowed her head, folded her hands, and started to pray: "Lord, thou preparest a table before me in the presence of mine enemies!"

Humorous? Yes, but I'm afraid that it is an all-too-clear picture of the attitude of many of the younger generation of our day. They have the feeling that those who restrain them are the enemy and are therefore to be opposed, intimidated, threatened, and overcome. It is a sad degeneration in the relationship between children and parents. As a recent TV series on the generation gap indicates, we have reached a time unprecedented in the history of our country, a time when understanding between parents and children is imperative as never before. Let us look therefore at what Scripture has to say about this.

Our text is taken from Ephesians, chapter 6, where we read something about the relationship and responsibilities of children and of parents. God speaks first to the children: "Children, obey your parents in the Lord: for this is right. Honor thy father and mother; which is the first commandment with promise; that it may be well with thee, and thou mayest live long on the earth." The first responsibility of a child is very simple: "Obey your parents in the Lord." The phrase "in the Lord" modifies "obey"; this means that children are to obey in the Lord not only Christian parents but unconverted ones as well.

Unless children are "in the Lord" they are not likely to be naturally submissive and obedient to their parents. But even natural morality would show that in the very nature of things, in the very organization of the universe, it is right and proper that children should obey their parents. Their parents are wiser and more experienced, and have been given to them by God to protect them, to train them, and to rear them up in the Lord. Therefore they are to be obeyed. The Apostle goes on to say that the first commandment God has given with promise is that children are to honor their father and their mother. We mentioned that though the wife is to be in subjection to her husband, the Bible never commands the husband to subject his wife to himself. The husband's responsibility is to *love* his wife. The wife's responsibility is to *subject herself* to her husband. But in this case it is the children's responsibility to *obey their parents.* In many other places we are told that it is the parents' responsibility to see that they do so. A number of biblical passages instruct us in training the child, correcting the child, and chastening the child, for as God chastens every son whom he receives, so the parents are to chasten their children.

The Bible says, "He that spareth the rod hateth his son." Also, "Chasten your child while there is yet hope." The Bible says that we are to use the rod and to spare not, for the child will not die. We are not to cease because of his crying. It is very interesting to note that God says that a parent who loves his child will chasten him with the rod. And the parent who does not chasten his child hates his child, knowingly or unknowingly. This is pretty strong language but God said it. It says that if we use the rod, we will deliver our child from hell. Isn't that an awesome responsibility? The child must learn to submit himself to a higher authority while he is still young. If he does not learn this as a child, he will most likely never learn as an adult to submit himself to the authority of Jesus Christ as Lord and Master.

For the past thirty or thirty-five years in this country we have been led into a permissive generation by prominent psychologists and educators. We were told that spanking a child was certainly a barbaric and uncivilized way for an intelligent modern to act, and that God certainly never meant for us to spank our children or to discipline them physically! Of course, children are not to be mistreated. This would be a great crime in the sight of God, for no parent has unlimited control over his child. Certainly no parent has a right to take the life of his child. Punishment is to be meted out in love.

But these leaders told us the thing to do was to be permissive with children and to bring out all that was in them. We have succeeded in doing this! Of course, we have ignored the words of Christ, who said that out of the heart proceed murders, adulteries, lusting, hate, lying, evil, and every type of wicked work! This is what we have brought out of our children! We live in a time where we are seeing our little Frankenstein monsters come of age. In large cities many people don't go out on the streets at night because we have created a whole new generation of people who care nothing at all for authority. All of this began in the home.

It began with parents who were more inclined to believe ungodly teachers and psychologists than the Word of God. Or with parents who were not willing to have their ease disturbed with such onerous tasks as administering discipline, but would rather let the boat remain unrocked in order to keep things peaceful. They didn't like to hear the crying! Someone has said, "What we have today is not a generation gap but a discipline gap."

The first duty of a child is to obey his parents, and the first duty of a parent is to discipline his child. All authority is given from God. We are placed under the authority of men so that we may learn how to live under the authority of God. Unfortunately, we have taught our children just the opposite by our lives. I wonder how many mothers have lamented the disobedience of their children but have been unwilling to subject themselves to their husbands. Or how many husbands have lamented their wives' insubordination and their children's rebelliousness, but have themselves been unwilling to submit to their head, who is Christ. There is such a thing as rebellious parents as well as rebellious children.

One writer recently stated that most parents today have at least learned that they can't let children go around throwing temper tantrums everytime they want something. Otherwise, when the child sees something he wants in a department store he will scream, fall on the floor, kick his heels, and bang his head against the floor until he finally gets what he wants. This could create a very difficult situation, making it hard to continue shopping over the thrashing bodies of all of these children in the aisles!

We know that this is not right, but we have not followed through with our discipline, so what we have is a whole generation of teen-agers throwing temper tantrums on college campuses. But they are a little bigger now, and instead of beating their heels against the floor they are beating meat cleavers against presidents' desks as they make their demands!

I think that young and old alike need to hear what God says about disobedience and rebellion; what he says to both parents and children; what he says to those who practice rebellion and to those who allow it. We have come to a time in our society where the whole fabric of society is being torn apart by rebellion in our cities and on our college campuses. "Woe unto the rebellious child, saith the Lord." Over and over again God speaks to those who have been rebellious, and his word is that stiff-necked rebellion is as the sin of witchcraft — an abomination in his sight. That is the message that America needs to hear today.

The other message is this: the only reason our young people are rebelling the way they are today is that adults are allowing it. They are not only allowing it; they are condoning it. Some are applauding it! A recent Presidential Commission report indicates that some adults are even organizing youth rebellion!

God has much to say about parents who allow this type of thing to continue. I am afraid that it is going to continue to happen in this country until we adults come to our senses and realize that it is our responsibility to stop it. That is the only way it is going to be stopped. And this stopping needs to begin with the child in the home. It needs to be continued in the school. Even if it means that older teen-agers will have to be locked up in jail, it is going to have to be *stopped*. It *must* be stopped, not only for the continuance of this nation, but for the salvaging of the child, for unless the impenitent, proud, hardhearted rebel comes to see his sin and repents of it, that child is doomed forever. "He that spareth the rod hateth his son."

I think that we as parents need to make abundantly clear to our children at home both their and our responsibility before God. We need to make clear to our teachers and to our schools, just how we feel about this matter. As long as we remain silent we will be like Eli, who pampered his children and brought them and himself down to destruction.

I am sometimes amazed at the limitless confidence which some of our younger rebels have in their own wisdom. They are absolutely sure that their elders have been immoral, unprincipled, and unloving, and that they alone have suddenly invented virtue! This vast and pompous assertion of their own infallibility would be laughable if it were not such a tragedy. Many of these young rebels, with only the barest taste of Bible knowledge, will even exhibit the presumption of backing their self-righteous protests with Scriptures twisted out of context, ill-understood, and wrongly used.

For example, the protests against war, the repeated pious cries that war is unchristian, come from ignorant minds that have never so much as read through the New Testament, much less the whole Bible. If they would take the time, they would find that not all killing is murder — that the Scriptures forbid murder but command killing in certain cases. They would find that God demands that "he who sheds man's blood, by man shall his blood be shed" . . . that there are two Hebrew words and two Greek words for killing (one meaning murder and one meaning to kill in a just situation) . . . that God commands the State to take life under certain circumstances . . . that God commands the State to defend its citizens and to protect its peace both from hoodlums within and enemies without. But despite their ignorance of Scripture they still have the audacity to throw up their cliches to support their rebellion, when the truth is that they have learned to be rebels from their youth. They have a contempt for all authority, and for God most of all. "Chasten them while there is yet hope."

Another responsibility of the child and the parents is that of learning and nurture. The parent is commanded by God to nurture the child, to teach him. "When he rises up . . . as they walk in the way . . . in his downsittings and his uprisings" — this is how he is to be taught. These words are to be whispered in his ear, line upon line, precept upon precept, here a little and there a little. The Word of God is to be *taught*. This is why we have a generation of young people who don't know anything about the Bible. They don't know the gospel. They don't have eternal life. They are afraid of dying. One of the basic reasons behind their protests is that they are afraid of death. They are terrified by the thought of war and the prospect of dying because they have never come to the assurance of eternal life.

Most parents have failed to systematically, day by day instruct their children in the Scriptures. We have turned them over to the Sunday school, not realizing that seventy-five years ago, when the Sunday school was in its infancy, it was intended for children with no parents or with ungodly parents. Good Christian parents taught their children at home, and taught them so much that they didn't feel any need for an organized school on Sunday. But this has changed now, and in many cases we have turned over the whole burden of the spiritual education of our children to the Sunday school teacher, who tries to do in one hour on Sunday what the parents should have been doing all week long. We are to *teach* them the Word of God. We are to help them to learn it, to hide it in their hearts.

If your child has a problem with stealing, have him memorize a half dozen verses of what God says about stealing. If your child is a liar, teach him to memorize God's word that says, "No liar shall be admitted into the kingdom of Heaven." I guarantee you that God's Spirit will take that Word and use it in the child's life. If your child has a problem with impurity, teach him what God has to say about this. If your child has a problem with discipline, teach him what God says about chastening and disciplining. Have your child read for himself what God says about discipline: *"He that spareth the rod hateth his son; but he that loveth him chasteneth him betimes."* God's Word will have a tremendous effect upon the child's life.

Unfortunately, too often what we teach our children directly is contradicted by what we teach them indirectly. One young child was asked "Do you have prayers in your home?" "Yes," he said. They asked, "When?" He replied, "When company comes!" The only thing this child is being taught is that God is the God of public opinion.

Andrew Murray, that famous minister from South Africa, had four brothers and three sisters in his family. Each one of them turned out to be a most outstanding individual. One day his mother was asked how she managed to raise seven of the most marvelous children that had ever graced that state. She said that her only secret was to live before them exactly the kind of life she wanted them to live.

What kind of lives are we living before our children? Are we showing them an example of love, of kindness, of virtue, of peace, of thoughtfulness? Or are we showing them an example of irritability and deceitfulness? The child steals a lollipop and gets a spanking. Then he washes his hands and dries them on a Hilton towel!

We are to discipline our children; we are to nurture them; we are to love them. Parents are to love their children and children are to love their parents. Not only does the Bible say, "Children, *obey* your parents," but it also says, "Children, *honor* your parents," which goes beyond obedience.

Parents, when we administer discipline let us be consistent. This is the most important factor in giving discipline. Let us also be *loving* in our administration of discipline. How sad it is to see the horrible misuse of discipline in which parents allow their child to become nearly uncontrollable, then lose their temper and strike the child in the face. Discipline must be administered both lovingly and regularly.

Never does a child need more to be assured of your love than when you discipline him. Instead of chasing him from you, let the child know that you love him, before and after you discipline him. Think back in your own childhood. Do you remember the spankings? Do you remember whether your parents told you why they were doing it? Perhaps they were doing it for wrong reasons. Perhaps it was impatience, or anger, or loss of temper, or perhaps they were doing it for the right reasons but never really told you so.

Over and over again we need to let our children know that we are disciplining them because we love them.

Phillip Henry wrote in his diary, "We have been married twenty years today and have never been reconciled because we have never needed to be reconciled. Twenty years and twenty thousand blessings the Lord has bestowed upon us." They had a home where *love prevailed*. Into this home was born Matthew Henry, who became such a saintly expositor of the Scriptures that Thomas Chalmer said he read Matthew Henry's writings on his knees, so close did they bring him to the throne of grace.

May God in his grace raise up families where children love their parents and parents love their children. Where children honor their parents and parents discipline their children in love.

"Parents, provoke not your children to wrath, but bring them up in the nurture and admonition of the Lord. Children, honor your father and your mother, that it may be well with thee, and that thy days may be long upon the earth."

Wives without Warmth

Recently somebody told me that sexual incompatibility shouldn't be a problem for anyone: all we really need is a proper division of labor — the husband provides the "income" and the wife provides the "patibility"! This humorous assessment of the marriage relationship points up a basic problem which some of us face: *we don't want to think about the true responsibility of sex in Christian marriage.* Yet it is a subject which we desperately need to explore.

Parents, the world is speaking on this subject. Its voice is loud and clear and usually depraved; yet it is constantly being heard by our children. You think you have protected them? They could tell you more about the facts of life than you yourself know! And at ages you wouldn't believe! Shall we let the world speak out, and not the Bible? Shall we let the devil speak, and not God? This is just what has happened, I'm afraid, on the part of many people. They have become so confused by all the turmoil over the subject, their minds have become so rattled by it all, that some have tried to censor God. This is prudery at its height. How can depraved and fallen man have the gall to throttle the Word of God! The Bible has a great deal to say about the subject of sex, and it has never been more urgently needed than now.

I think one reason for this confusion is that so much of the talk about sex has a false, materialistic, antiscriptural, and anti-Christian basis. In fact I would venture to say that this is true of 98 percent of the talk our children hear on the subject. Shall we let them hear nothing else? I think there was never a time when our children more urgently needed to hear some good, wholesome, scriptural teaching on this subject, and many adults as well. Let me go on record as saying that I am unequivocally opposed to a great deal of the discussion of sex that is rampant in our country today, for the simple reason that it promotes sinfulness, licentiousness, and sexual immorality. Most of what is taught muddies the water, confuses the subject, and makes ten times more difficult the ministers' responsibility to speak out on the biblical teaching about sex.

I am convinced that in no other area has Satan achieved such resounding success as in the area of sex. This has been one of his greatest victories, and has produced unspeakable misery in individuals and homes. It has seriously weakened the Christian home — the very foundation of the church. Tens of millions of Christians around the world are unable to serve Christ properly or witness effectively to the grace of God in their lives, because they are continually defeated in their lives at home, in their efforts to be husbands and wives. There is a great need for something to be done in this area. One divorce judge who listened to marital problems for over thirty years, reported that in the overwhelming majority of divorce cases in America, the basic underlying cause was sexual incompatibility. This has led to the most phenomenal divorce rate in the history of mankind! Is there a need for biblical sex education? I think there is!

Clinical studies have shown that 40 to 50 percent of American women are suffering from some form or some degree of the hypoesthetic syndrome commonly called frigidity. This means that 40,000,000 American women are suffering from either a minor inability to fully enjoy marriage or else a complete absence of any sexual feelings at all. This, the studies show, has produced a soaring divorce rate, broken homes, delinquent children, homosexuality, fornication, adultery, and general disorder in the social realm. If you could sit with me behind a pastoral counseling desk and hear the cries of anguish from men and women who have suffered for years with sexual problems, you would know how great the need is. You would hear men say that they wake up in the night, look at their wives, and despise them. You would hear women say that their marriage has turned out to be an arid wasteland or a horrible nightmare.

How did we arrive at this situation? Let us look at some facts. During the past thirty years a tremendous amount of clinical and scientific study has been given to this problem. Certain facts have emerged which are astonishing to many of us. In the last ten years facts have been uncovered that were completely unknown when I studied the subject in seminary — things that some readers may be totally unfamiliar with. It is likely that some of you reading these words hold erroneous ideas about this matter of sexual relations and adjustment in marriage.

Before we look at what the Bible has to say about this subject, consider two contrasting aberrations. Materialism says, in effect, that man is simply matter in motion, that he has no soul or spirit, that he is not immortal, that he is simply a very clever animal, that sex is simply for sensual enjoyment, that there is no God, that marriage is an unnecessary evil, that children should be avoided if possible and endured if necessary, that promiscuity should be encouraged, and that homosexuality should be discussed and practiced. This type of materialistic thinking is found in every area of our country today. It can be seen on television, in all sorts of talk shows and interviews. It is seen in innumerable magazines and novels. It permeates the motion pictures. Your children are imbued with it already.

At the opposite extreme is the ascetic heresy. Asceticism teaches that man is basically spirit; that only spirit is good and that matter and flesh are therefore evil. Sex is regarded as particularly evil. This view says that sex should never be discussed and should be avoided if at all possible; that perhaps it must be endured by some in marriage, the less the better. Like materialism, the ascetic heresy has done incalculable damage in our time.

The Bible, however, teaches something entirely different. In the very first chapter of Scripture we read that God in the beginning created man in his own image. He created mankind as male and female. God looked upon all that he created and saw that it was very good. And God commanded that for this reason a man should cleave to his wife, and they would become one flesh. This is the first scriptural teaching on the subject. Let us see what is involved. First we note that *God* made man and woman, male and female. God made *two* sexes — not one. He saw that it was *good,* which means that the maleness of the man and the femaleness of the woman are *good.*

Dr. Marie Robinson, a medical doctor, psychiatrist, and psychoanalyst who has made in-depth studies in this area, says that much of the problem which exists in our time is sociologically produced and much of it has to do with women. But it is not the average woman's fault. In fact it is not woman's fault that she is frigid. This is something that was produced in her as a child, in most cases, by the society in which she lived, and usually by her mother. The reason this type of problem is most often found among women is a biological one, concludes Dr. Robinson, for nature has so arranged things that anything that has to do with the perpetuation of the species is carefully guarded against harm. The sexuality of a man is essential to the perpetuation of the human race, but the ability to enjoy sexual pleasure is unnecessary to a woman for the perpetuation of the human species. A woman may be, as Dr. Robinson said, as frigid as a polar icecap, yet give birth to twenty-five children, hate every minute of it, and make her husband, herself, and her children miserable in the process!

But because it is not essential to the continuance of the species, the sexual enjoyment of a woman is a very fragile thing. Like a small tree planted with very fragile roots, the winds of error and heresy can destroy that tree. This has been done in America to an amazing degree, leaving millions of women deprived of their birthright, miserable in their marriages, unfulfilled as women, and quite anxious about what I am saying. How did this come about? Dr. Robinson points out that the essential sociological factors are two in number. To understand them, she says, we must go back at least two hundred years into our environment to see what has produced this. At that time in America the home was the center of activity. Most homes were rural. The cities had only begun to develop. The mother was the center of the home life. The children were reared at her knee. There was no public education. The children were taught not only reading, writing, and arithmetic, but all the other things they would need to know, right in the home. The woman worked side by side as a full partner with her husband. She enjoyed her role as woman. Though her life was hard, she nevertheless never doubted her importance. She never minimized her role as the mother of her children. To be a wife for her husband was a high calling indeed — one which was thoroughly appreciated by both husband and children. Frigidity was almost unheard of in those days.

But then something happened. A man by the name of James Watt developed the steam engine. Unrelated? Listen to this: the steam engine produced the Industrial Revolution, the Industrial Revolution produced the city, and the city revolutionized the home. No longer was the home the center of activities. No longer was the husband working side by side with his wife. Instead, he was gone most of the day working in the city, making more money than he ever did before. The children were gone to public schools now, to be educated by others. No longer was it essential for the mother to bake the bread — it could be bought in any store. Her whole role in life was stripped from her, and her whole feminine nature was devalued. She seemed no longer needed. She was no longer an equal partner with her husband. She found herself dispossessed.

The woman reacted, says Dr. Robinson, in a decisive act of rage.

It began with what was known as the feminist movement. In 1794, less than thirty years after the Industrial Revolution, Mary Wollstonecraft wrote a book entitled *The Vindication of the Rights of Woman.* The rights of women were being taken away, she wrote. Women must react! Rise, women of the world, and assert yourselves! If your femaleness is going to be looked down upon, we will react! We will enter into the realm of men! We will compete with men! We will supersede men! We will, in effect, *become* men.

Does this sound familiar? For over 150 years the principles of the feminist movement have controlled the thinking of millions of Americans. Today almost every single detail set forth in Mary Wollstonecraft's book has been fulfilled. Yet women were never more miserable than they are today. Never were more homes in agony than today. Never has there been more frustration and less fulfillment than there is in the modern American home.

Another movement was taking place at the same time, but much more quietly. It was not by the vociferous woman, epitomized by the flapper of the twenties, but by the Victorian woman, the quiet woman who remained in the home. Her reaction was, "If femaleness is depreciated, I will simply become anti-sexual." And so she did. She said that sexuality was simply a male propensity and that "we finer women really had none of it." These women even convinced many a doctor and author at the turn of the century that women do not have sexual desires. Still today some people hold these views.

During the last thirty years the light of science has turned toward this area. There has been an overwhelming amount of examination done in this field from various scientific disciplines. One of the incontestable facts brought to light is this: a woman is absolutely as sexual as a man; in her normal state she has every bit as much sexual desire as any man. Have you been deceived? Satan has deceived millions of women. Let me make one thing clear. This is no attack on women. God loves women. I love them for Christ's sake. And I am angered that Satan has deceived them, and robbed them of their birthright, and stripped them of their fulfillment of womanhood.

Satan works in devious ways. He attacks people where they are weakest. As I have said before, men tend less than women to seek after God and spiritual things, because Christ has so blessed women. There is many a godly wife with an ungodly husband. Satan hits women in their weak point by robbing them of their sexuality through psychological blockage. Satan has produced millions of homes with spiritless men and sexless women, where "home" is hell on earth. Paul said, "We are not ignorant of his [Satan's] devices" — but *we* are colossally ignorant of them! And we reap his bitter rewards.

Oh, that men would see that sex is a high and holy privilege and that it must be bathed in the pure light of the Spirit of God. Oh, that they would approach it in a tender and compassionate way, so that they can enter into the fullness of joy that God meant for their homes. Oh, that women would see that they have been deceived by the devil and robbed of their inherent birthright by creation.

Let me give you a word of encouragement. Help is available. Almost every case of sexual incompatibility can be cured. It is my hope that you will see something of the nature and the gravity of the problem and some of the causes. Most of all, it is my desire that you will find new hope. May this come as a bright and shining star into dark homes that have long ago given up hope. Whoever you are, there is help for you. I hope that you will seek it. Often simply a helpful book or a skillful counselor can unlock doors that have long been locked in a woman's heart. Many are easily led to the fulfillment of what is theirs by birthright.

I pray that each of you will seek the physical and spiritual ideals that God has designed for us; that our homes should be places of true love, places where competition and animosity and fear and guilt and envy are removed and where two partners can enter into that communion of love, that oneness of flesh and spirit that God meant for us to have. If this is not yours now, then seek it. If you do not seek it you are sinning against God, against your husband or wife, against your children, and against yourself.

Lincoln the Mountain Climber

"The world will little note nor long remember what we say here,
But it can never forget what they did here.
It is for us, the living, rather to be dedicated here to the unfinished work which they who fought here have thus far so nobly advanced . . .
That this nation, under God, shall have a new birth of freedom;
And that government of the people, by the people, and for the people
Shall not perish from the earth."

These immortal words of Abraham Lincoln have gained him the everlasting honor of Americans. Statesmen the world around will always admire the nobility of Lincoln's character and the selflessness of his actions. Truly the spirit of Lincoln lives forever!

Yet these enduring memories of Lincoln pale beside the more crucial question: Did Lincoln have eternal *life?* And the most crucial question faces each reader of this message: Do *you* have eternal life?

Was Lincoln a true Christian? It seems that there is a difference of opinion. His first biography presents him as a skeptic and an unbeliever, lacking any true faith. He never joined any church. Yet Wordsworth says that he had a faith of the profoundest type. Father Chiniquy, a former Roman priest, says that Lincoln was the perfect type of Christian. What a paradox! How can a man be at the same time an unbeliever and the perfect type of Christian?

This question deserves our attention, for it may shed light on the most crucial question of all: Do *I* truly have eternal life?

In the year 1806 evangelist Peter Cartwright was holding revival meetings in the backwoods of Kentucky. From the circle of bowed heads a young man leaped to his feet, shouting with joy and dancing round the camp. Moments later a young lady followed suit, singing for joy and leaping around the circle. Who were these two young people? They were Tom Lincoln and Nancy Hanks; with their wedding date only a week away they were rededicating their lives to their Lord. In 1809 they gave birth to a son, giving him the biblical name of Abraham. Such was the spiritual atmosphere in which the sixteenth President of our United States began his life.

Preacher and author F. W. Boreham describes the early years of Lincoln's life as the "Iron Age." It was during this time that Lincoln climbed the first of three "mountains." "Mount Sinai — with Moses" aptly describes these formative years of Lincoln's life, for it was during these days that young Abe sat on his godly mother's knee and listened to the Ten Commandments from the Holy Scriptures. During later years Lincoln could recount that these were among his most treasured moments of boyhood, and that these biblical teachings never ceased having a profound effect on his daily life behavior. Though Abe's mother died when he was only nine years old, the mature Lincoln was known to repeat with fondness, "All that I am I owe to my angel-mother." This was the kind of legacy Nancy Lincoln left her son.

As a young man Lincoln pursued an exceedingly honest life. As a struggling lawyer he would remind his opponents of points they had forgotten in their cases. He would defend the poor free of charge. To every bribe he responded with a flat refusal. He soon became known as the most honest lawyer east of China! Even today we know him as 'Honest Abe'. When asked about his honesty Lincoln replied, "Whenever I am confronted with some temptation, I can still vividly hear in my mind the tones of my mother's voice saying, 'I am the Lord thy God, which have brought thee out of the land of Egypt . . . Thou shalt not steal!' "

Lincoln had a high regard for the Lord's day and disapproved of any unnecessary work on that day. This is illustrated by an event that took place during the war, while Lincoln was President. During the President's visit to Falmouth, General McDowell told Lincoln that he would be able to start his march to Richmond on Sunday, but, knowing the President's objection to initiating movement on that day, he would leave it to his judgment. Lincoln's reply was, "Take a good rest and start Monday morning." Truly here was a man who tried to keep the commandments of God!

He was in fact a remarkable man in many ways. Just the mention of his name brings his startling appearance before us: six-feet-four-inch frame . . . fantastically long arms and gigantic hands (the utter frustration of his tailors) . . . long legs . . . tall and somewhat beaten top hat . . . long black coat . . . black shawl on his shoulders . . . sallow cheeks . . . deep, sunken, melancholy eyes . . . high cheekbones . . . the shock of hair uncontrollable upon his head!

Abraham Lincoln — a man of diverse talents! After studying the life of Lincoln for many years I was surprised to find that Lincoln was a weightlifter! In addition, he was an acknowledged wrestling champion and an exceptionally capable runner.

Lincoln grew up in a religious atmosphere. He attended church in Indiana at the Pigeon Creek Baptist Church. What a plain church — just a bucket of water at one end and a stove at the other, with a simple pulpit holding a big Bible, and behind it a preacher who believed this Bible and preached it! Little Abe would come to church with Sally Bush, his stepmother, and her daughter Sarah, each child sitting on one side of the mother. There they sat — Abraham and Sarah! Lincoln was familiar with the words of Scripture. He knew such words as foreordination, predestination, the gospel, justification, the new birth, evangelism, sanctification, adoption, and many others. "If ever a man had eternal life," we would say, "it was the young man Abraham Lincoln." Yet for all of Lincoln's outstanding personal character, the evidence shows that he had not yet truly received Christ as his Savior.

Boreham describes the second phase of Lincoln's life as the "age of clay" — the moldable years, where he climbed Mount Carmel with Elijah and found that God answered by fire. This was the period when he was going into politics. His life was being transformed and fused by the power of God and the fires of the struggles into which he was plunged. He was going to Washington. On his way someone sent him a flag with the following words inscribed on it: "Be strong and of a good courage; be not afraid, neither be thou dismayed: for the Lord thy God is with thee withersoever thou goest." These words, spoken first to Joshua, became a source of limitless courage to Lincoln. As he went from Springfield to Washington he said that he went forth in the name of the Lord God Almighty! He believed that God was with him as he had been with Washington, and that he was indestructible until his task was finished. With such words he found his slow way to Washington and to the presidency.

Now what kind of a man was he personally — this young man who grew up in the back woods? He was described as unattractive. In fact, when he was born someone said, "Tom and Nancy have the ugliest child I ever saw." One day, when he was President, Lincoln looked in the mirror and said, "It's a fact, Abe! You are the ugliest man in the world. If I ever see a man uglier than you I'm going to shoot him on the spot!" Lincoln was described during this period as unattractive, illiterate, self-opinionated, overbearing, and abominably ill-mannered. Does that surprise you? Young Abraham Lincoln not only didn't have good looks, but he didn't have education, he didn't have good manners, he didn't have anything! One day a lady told him just that — that he was totally lacking in all of those fine graces that make a man appealing to a woman!

And so Lincoln set out to amend his character. He turned to the Word of God in order to find the strength to change his life. He was clay in the hands of the Lord. How successful was he? This illiterate man became not only exceedingly literate but undoubtedly one of the finest orators that the world has ever seen.

The imagery of his speeches is beautiful to envision. His imagination was tremendous. Who else would have pictured our beloved country as a newborn child, growing in strength: "Fourscore and seven years ago, our fathers brought forth upon this continent a new nation, conceived in liberty, and dedicated to the proposition that all men are created equal. . . ." This speech is said to be the most perfect that has ever been uttered. He became so polished that he was considered to be the most complete gentleman any society could desire. His winsomeness was tremendous. During Lincoln's bid for the presidency the common saying was, "He has no education; he has no great accomplishments in the past; all he has are friends everywhere!" This is what happened to our ill-mannered boor!

Lincoln became an exceedingly humble man. He had a little couplet on humility that he used to repeat over and over:

> "O why should the spirit of a mortal be proud?
> Like a fleeting meteor, or a passing cloud,
> A flash of lightning, or the break of a wave,
> It passes from life, to rest in the grave."

Lincoln found in the Scriptures the power to mold and transform his life. To the honesty he had practiced from his youth he added courtesy, humility, and vision. Yet something was still missing. Ward Lamon, Lincoln's personal bodyguard, had this to say about him: "The misery that dripped from Lincoln as he walked was caused by his lack of any personal religious faith." How can this be? How can the great Abraham Lincoln be said to lack religious faith? Surely there must be a sense in which Lincoln believed in the Commandments of God and indeed in God himself.

Yes, there is a sense in which Lincoln believed in God. Lincoln could see *God working in the affairs of men.* He could see God's hand working everywhere. For example, why did Lincoln go into the law profession? It was because in the providence of God, while rummaging around in an old barrel of rubbish in his store at Salem, that he came upon a copy of Blackstone's *Commentaries,* and from that chance discovery were awakened the ambitions and desires which were to play so great a part in American history. Lincoln saw in this the providential hand of God. Again, why did Lincoln issue the Emancipation Proclamation when he did? On January 1, 1863, Lincoln had called his cabinet together. He pulled out of his old black, battered hat a small white piece of paper on which was scribbled the first draft of the Emancipation Proclamation. He said, "I made a solemn vow to the Lord that if he granted us victory at Antietam that I would emancipate the slaves." He threw the paper on the table. There was no hint of political expediency or military usefulness. It was a vow to God, and since God's hand had been obvious in the battle of Antietam he would fulfill his vow. He went forth, as Joshua did, in the strength of the Lord. You see, he had a *providential* faith. He had a faith for *temporal* things. He believed that God would protect him until his task was done. He believed that God would guide him in the job that was left to him. And yet, friend, *this is not a saving faith!* Lincoln was still a lost man. "The misery that dripped from him," as Ward Lamon said, "was from his lack of personal religious faith."

Lincoln's third phase in his spiritual development is described by Boreham as the "golden age" — the age when Lincoln climbed Mount Calvary with John. Theodore Roosevelt said that Abraham Lincoln mastered one book, and that book was the Bible. He read it incessantly, giving him the reputation of the most religious President that we have ever had. Before Calvary, however, there came Gethsemane — sorrow, public and private. The public sorrow was his sorrow over the war. For years I have been fascinated by this man as I have read about his life and writings. Over and over again my heart has been touched and I have been moved to tears by the tremendous concern he had for his country and for the young men who were dying in the war. When a general would come and give an account of a battle, he would become so agitated at hearing about the loss of life that he would pace up and down the room. And it seemed sometimes as if he would be beside himself with grief because of the loss of these soldiers. Over and over again he was seen praying. Many times during the Civil War he would pray all night long: "O God, I cannot lead this people. O God, unless thou dost help us, we shall have no victory. O God, help me. There is nothing I can do. I am but a poor, ignorant man. Thou, Lord, must help."

One night his friends left him sitting by the fireplace, his elbows on his knees and his face in his hands. They came back the following morning to find him still in the same position. As they stepped quietly into the room they could hear him praying in agonizing tones over and over again, "O God, O God, if it be possible let this cup pass from me." One Sunday, late at night, there was a knock at the door of Henry Ward Beecher, the famed minister of the Park Street Church of Boston. Rousing himself from his bed, Dr. Beecher went to the door to find a strange phenomenon facing him. There in the doorway stood a tall man so wracked with pain and sorrow as to be unrecognizable at first. After a few moments the minister realized that there, standing at his door in the middle of the night, was the President. He ushered him into his house. Lincoln, with shoulders stooped, sat on the edge of a chair and after a long silence said, "I think I shall never be glad again." His concern for the dying soldiers was beyond words.

President Wilson once said that he had read many of Lincoln's biographies and had sought out with great interest the intimate details of his life, but added, "I have nowhere found a real intimate of Lincoln's. That brooding spirit had no real familiars. I get the impression that it never spoke out in complete revelation and that it could not reveal itself completely to anyone. It was a lonely spirit that looked out from underneath those shaggy brows and comprehended men without fully communing with them as if, in spite of all of its genial efforts at comradeship, it dwelt apart; saw its visions of duty where no man looked on."

But his sorrow was not only public; it was also private. His son, the apple of his eye, the delight and joy of his life, was stricken with a severe illness. Day after day he stood watch by his bed with the nurse. Toward the end he became so anxious and so overwhelmed that when the boy finally died the nurse said she thought that Lincoln was going to go completely out of his mind. It seemed as though he could never again continue his work. Every Thursday he observed a whole day of mourning in remembrance of the death of his son, giving himself to nothing else. Lincoln was consumed with grief.

But the nurse who stood with Lincoln during these hours of agony was a Christian. During this wave of grief she pointed Lincoln toward the Cross and toward her Savior.

Shortly after this Lincoln went to Gettysburg. There, as he viewed the thousands upon thousands of crosses marking the graves of the war dead, he came face to face with Christ. He wrote these words in a letter to a friend: "When I came to Springfield, I was not a Christian. When I left Springfield for Washington and asked you to pray for me, I was not a Christian. When I went to Gettysburg, I was not a Christian. But there at Gettysburg I consecrated my heart to Christ."

Do you remember the words of Lincoln's Gettysburg Address: "It is for us, the living, rather, to be *dedicated here . . .*" Did you notice the phrases? "That this nation, under God, shall have a *new birth . . .*" He who had freed the slaves was there freed from the shackles of his sins and found the *new birth* that comes to those that *trust in Jesus Christ.*

Yes, Lincoln had tried to stagger up Mount Sinai carrying the huge burden of the Law with him. He had tried to transform his life into acceptance with God. He had trusted the Lord for the *temporal things* of life. *But he had never trusted Christ for his salvation!* There at Gettysburg, through the war and the death of his son, he was brought to the end of himself, and he surrendered his life to Christ. He yielded himself to the Savior. Later he said that for years he had sought a more personal faith, and that he had found it as he climbed Mount Calvary and found the Cross. This was his true birthday! Abraham Lincoln's birthday should be celebrated on November 19, for on that day in the year 1863 *Lincoln became a Christian!*

Boreham says, "With tears in his eyes he told his friends that he had at last found the faith that he had longed for. He realized, he said, that his heart was changed and that he loved the Savior. The President was at the Cross!"

Further evidence of Lincoln's conversion to Christ was recently uncovered when the New York Presbyterian Church of Washington, D.C., where Lincoln was a regular attendant, discovered in its archives a letter signed by President Lincoln shortly before his death. The letter states that he had given a great deal of thought to the question of his soul's salvation, and was now ready to make a public confession of his faith in Jesus Christ as his Savior. The letter was dated Tuesday, April 13, 1865. His reception into the church was set for Sunday, April 18, 1865.

But barely twenty-four hours after he signed this letter there rang through the Ford Theatre the "maddest pistol shot in the history of the ages." And Abraham Lincoln was baptized, not with water but with blood.

Yet here is his public profession for all the world to see and to emulate: "I then and there consecrated my heart to Christ."

Though he was not to live long thereafter, the events of those last days contain incidents worthy of our careful notice.

Lincoln's words to Congress concerning the destiny of the nation to be uniquely fulfilled in his own life and death. He said, "Fellow citizens, we cannot escape history. We of this Congress and this administration will be remembered in spite of ourselves. No personal significance or insignificance can spare one or another of us. The fiery trial through which we pass will light us down in honor or dishonor to the latest generation. We shall nobly save or meanly lose the last best hope of earth."

Lincoln was re-elected by an overwhelming vote. In his second inaugural address, coming from the heart of one whose sins had been forgiven, he could say, "With malice toward none, with charity toward all. . . ." Five weeks later Lee surrendered. Then came April, 1865. Abraham Lincoln had been a Christian one year and five months. He had said prophetically at the time of his second election, "I shall not live out this term. When this struggle is over my work on earth shall be done." The war ended. Lincoln staunchly opposed those who would demand the pound of flesh from the South, and defended a generous peace.

On the night of April 14, Lincoln went with his wife to the Ford Theatre. The play was almost over when they arrived. But he wasn't watching it. His wife Mary was at his side. Lincoln was leaning in his chair and talking to Mary. There was a lilt in his voice. The long war and struggle was over. The victory was won. The Union was secured.

Would you like to know the last words that Lincoln uttered on that fateful night? He said, "Mary, you know what I would like most of all in the world to do? I would like to take you with me on a trip to the Near East. We could go to Palestine. We could visit Bethlehem where he was born." John Wilkes Booth stepped into the box. "We could go to Nazareth . . . and Bethany." Booth lifted the gun to Lincoln's head. "And Mary," he continued, "we could go up to Jeru- . . ." A shot rang out! A bullet pierced his brain!

In a noble eulogy Bishop Simpson said, "Chieftain, farewell! The Nation mourns thee; mothers shall teach thy name to their lisping children; the youth of our land shall emulate thy virtues; statesmen shall study thy record and from it learn lessons of wisdom. Mute though thy lips be, yet they shall speak; hushed is thy voice, but its echoes of liberty are ringing through the world, and the sons of bondage listen with joy."

Perhaps the greatest expression of the heart-love of the people for Lincoln has been given by Walt Whitman, as Whitman watched the Ship of States, having come through the great storm of Civil War, now sailing grandly into port — with her Captain fallen on the deck:

"O Captain! my Captain! our fearful trip is done;
 The ship has weathered every rock, the prize we sought is won;
 The port is near, the bells I hear, the people all exulting,
 While follow eyes the steady keel, the vessel grim and daring:
             But O heart! heart! heart!
             O the bleeding drops of red,
             Where on the deck my Captain lies,
                 Fallen cold and dead.

O Captain! my Captain! rise up and hear the bells;
Rise up — for you the flag is flung — for you the bugle trills;
For you bouquets and ribbon's wreaths — for you the shores a-crowding;
For you they call, the swaying mass, their eager faces turning.
    Here Captain! dear father!

64

>   This arm beneath your head;
>   It is some dream that on the deck,
>   You've fallen cold and dead.
>
> My Captain does not answer, his lips are pale and still;
> My father does not feel my arm, he has no pulse nor will;
> The ship is anchor'd safe and sound, its voyage closed and done;
> From fearful trip, the victor ship, comes in with object won;
>   Exult, O shores, and ring, O bells!
>   But I, with mournful tread,
>   Walk the deck my Captain lies,
>   Fallen cold and dead."

But *we* cannot leave him there. May I add to Boreham's third mountain another peak. Lincoln climbed Mount Calvary with John. Ah, yes, but he climbed at last the heavenly Mount Jerusalem with Christ. He rose up because the Lord raised him up and he heard the bugles trill, he heard the bells ringing, and saw the faces exulting, as he was welcomed by an innumerable host into the New Jerusalem — which is above. For Lincoln trusted in the Christ who died for him, and so we know that *he is alive,* not merely in the memory of his countrymen but eternally in heaven with his Savior Jesus Christ!

Yes, Lincoln was indeed a Christian — are you?

What Are You Dying For?

What are you committed to? Perhaps you do not even know what it is, but you are surely committed to something! Young or old, man or woman, boy or girl, everyone is committed to something because that is the very nature of man. God made us to be committed to something. You say, "Why, I'm not committed to anything. I'm not carrying a banner for any great cause." Perhaps you fail to understand the meaning of the word. Whether you are a businessman burning yourself out for your business night and day, a housewife determined to keep up with the Joneses, a student determined to be at the top of his class, an athlete heading for the major leagues, an avid outdoorsman, or just a TV addict, *you are committed to something.*

Some people will commit themselves just as fully to avoiding work as others who work for a cause. Some commitments may be to things which are dramatic, spectacular, and revolutionary, things which attract the attention of all the world. Hitler's commitment to world dominion brought the attention of all of the world upon him. Then there are those who are committed to a life of ease and sufficiency, not having too much and not having too little, not really getting involved with anything other than me, my, and mine. This type of commitment isn't as obvious because it isn't famous or notorious. But it is just as real as the commit-

66

ment of Hitler, Caesar, Napoleon, or the Apostle Paul. We are all committed to something, somewhere. In the soul of every man incense burns to something. Deep down in the crypt of every heart someone or something wears a crown. Who wears your crown?

Let us look at the secret of commitment. It is not quite as simple as we sometimes think it is. Why are people committed to certain things rather than to others! How do we become committed? What is the secret of it? Let us consider a man who devoted years of his life to becoming an effective orator. He was committed to this task as few men have ever been committed to anything. He labored tirelessly for years to perfect his ability. Did he succeed? History is filled with the honor of his name as the greatest orator of all time. His name was Demosthenes.

Perhaps you recall the story. As a boy he was shy and diffident. He stuttered and had an additional speech impediment. While he was still a lad his parents died and left him a vast estate. But in those days in Greece you had to defend the right to your inheritance at a public meeting. Demosthenes stammered so much that he was not able to defend his inheritance, and thus lost it to someone else. He was so enraged by this disinheritance that he put the now-famous pebbles in his mouth and went down to the beach. There, over the roar of the ocean breakers, he perfected the skill which was to set Greece aflame.

Human beings have certain basic needs: the desire for food and drink, the desire for the praise of others, the desire for the respect of men, the desire for fame or power, the desire for money and what it can buy, the desire for sex. These basic urges of human nature impel many people to do what they do. These form an important part of the secret of commitment.

Often the matter of "chance" helps mold a person's life commitment. It might be a chance reading of a newspaper ad, a chance encounter with an influential businessman, or a chance opportunity to pursue an unanticipated goal. Then we look back and find we have spent forty-five years pursuing a commitment that seemingly started by chance!

Most important of all is the matter of a world view, a view of life. Most people don't develop this in a philosophy class; they develop it unconsciously, long before they get to high school. They absorb it from their surroundings. They learn it from their parents and their friends. This matter of a world view is so important in determining our life commitments that the factors of chance and human need, though important, are secondary to it. The tragedy of it all is that most of us never consciously think about where our view of life is taking us, and so we wander through life without any clear-cut aims at all.

We fall into this or that and then give our whole lives to it. Later we look back and say, "What am I doing? I've spent thousands of hours on this foolishness!" Plato said that an unexamined life is not worth living. If this is ture, most of our lives are not worth living, because surely most of them are unexamined.

Why did you do what you spent your life doing, or are doing right now? Sometimes a businessman tells me, "I give myself to my business. That is the most important thing in the world, and I give all of my energies to it. It absorbs the greatest amount of my time." I feel like saying to him, "Why?" I am sure he would look at me in utter astonishment! He would say, "Why? Man, that's the way it is! That's life! That's the way things are!" You see, he is simply expressing his world view: that the main point in life is getting ahead, making a living, earning money. One day he may wake up to discover that what he once considered the essential facts of existence are the very delusions of Satan, and that he himself has been deceived.

In C. S. Lewis's *Screwtape Letters,* Screwtape, the archdemon in hell, sends letters of instruction to his nephew, Wormwood. It is his job to get a particular Englishman safely home to Satan. Screwtape tells him, "Don't argue, for the adversary can argue all too well, but rather keep his mind upon the stream of things and call that 'reality,' but never let him ask what reality means."

What does reality really mean? Have you left God out of your thinking? Have you left Jesus Christ, the Lord of Glory, out of your reckoning? The Bible says, "Man's life consisteth not in the abundance of the things which he possesseth." You may wake up too late to discover that you have been completely wrong. Listen to the Word of God: "Come now, let us reason together, saith the Lord." Stop and think, and reason what life is all about. "For what is your life?" says the Scripture. "It is even a vapor, that riseth up and disappeareth . . . we are like the grass which groweth up; in the morning it flourisheth, and in the evening it is cut down and withereth."

Are you sure that your commitment of life is a wise choice? Maybe there is someone at your shoulder keeping your eyes on the stream of things until he can get you safely home to your father below! The worldly-wise man is so clever. He has his thoughts arranged so beautifully. His bank account is bulging. His portfolio is neatly ordered. Yet he doesn't know he is a fool if he has left God out of the picture.

The fascinating thing to me about this matter of commitment, the key to it all, is simply this: What does the Bible say about commitment? Think of a passage where the term is used. You will have to think long and hard, for it never uses the term. This is an interesting fact in itself. The verb does occur, usually in the sense of committing a transgression, such as "Thou shalt not commit adultery." But there are a few occasions when the verb form "commit" does occur and where it means to entrust to someone. For example, Jesus did not *commit* himself to any man, John tells us. God has *committed* to your trust the true riches, we read in Luke. Paul said, "To me is *committed* a ministry of uncircumcision."

In checking the Greek text I discovered that in every single case where the verb "commit" is used in the latter sense, it is the word which means believe. The Bible doesn't use the word "commitment"; it uses the word "faith." In reality they are the same. Not only in the Bible but in everyday life, what we believe is what we are committed to. Whatever you believe to be your highest good is the cause to which you are committed. If you believe your highest good is a life of ease, you will be committed to that. If you believe your highest good is getting money, you will be committed to that. If you believe your highest good is becoming famous, you will be committed to that. If you believe the highest good is to glorify God and enjoy him forever, you will be committed to that.

Do you believe in Jesus Christ? The Bible doesn't use the word "believe" in some strange and esoteric way which people cannot understand. It uses it in exactly the same way that you use it every day in the business and secular world. It simply means to take someone at his word. I might say to you now, "This room is on fire and in just a minute the roof will come down on your head!" Yet not one of you would believe me! How do I know? You haven't left the room yet!

Jesus Christ says, "I am he that was dead, and behold, I am alive . . . go ye into all the world and preach the gospel to every creature." Yet some of you prove that you don't believe this because you don't go. This is what the Bible means when it says that "faith without works is dead." It doesn't mean that we are saved by faith plus works, but it means that genuine faith will inevitably produce works. Faith without works is no faith at all. It is exactly the lack of faith that you had in my word when I told you the room is on fire!

I am sure there are multitudes of people who deceive themselves into thinking that they believe in Jesus Christ. But believing in him is taking him at his Word regarding salvation: "He that believeth on me shall never perish." Do you believe this? Do you know for certain that you are going to heaven? If you don't you do not truly believe Christ's promise. Jesus said, "He that believeth on me hath everlasting life." If you believe it, you have it. And if you have it, you will live like it, and you will rejoice in the blessed assurance of life eternal.

Jesus said, "All power is given unto me in heaven and in earth. Go ye into all the world and preach the gospel." If you truly believe that, you will do it. If you don't do it, you don't believe it. "In that day, Jesus said, I will say to many, depart from me, for I never knew you." If you do not believe that Jesus Christ died for you and paid for all of your sins; if you do not believe that he freely offers you the gift of eternal life; if you do not believe that Christ has risen from the dead; if you do not believe that he has overcome the power of death, then quit being a hypocrite. Eat, drink, and be merry! Burn your Bibles and forget the pious sham. Either you believe it or you don't.

But if you can look into the hole in the cemetery and smile, if you believe Christ when he said, "Behold, I am he that was dead and am alive forevermore," then you will be committed to him and you will do what he told you to do. If you believe it, you're committed to it. That, my friends, is the secret of commitment.

Watch this secret at work in the life of a Christian young man. Jim Elliott, who with four other missionaries was murdered by the spears of Auca Indians, wrote in his diary: "He makes his ministers to be a flame of fire. Am I ignitable? Deliver me from the dread asbestos of other things. Saturate me with the oil of thy Spirit, that I may be a flame. But flame is transient, often short-lived. Canst thou bear this, O my soul? Short life? But in me there dwells the Spirit of the great short-lived, whose zeal for his Father's house consumed him. Make me thy fuel, O flame of God." This is total life commitment. And what was it based upon? He believed in Jesus Christ, the great short-lived who had come to live in his heart. He knew that he would live forever with him.

This was the secret of commitment of the Apostle Paul, who could say, "But this one thing I do, forgetting those things which are behind, and reaching forth unto those things which are before, I press toward the mark for the prize of the high calling of God in Christ Jesus." He could truthfully say that he demonstrated that commitment in his life because he believed.

To what are you committed? Are you committed to some passing goal, a god that dies when life on earth is over? Or are you commited heart and soul to the Lord Jesus Christ, the everlasting God of heaven?

Happy Christians

Many people who have become Christians have found that the new life has been an exceedingly difficult experience, with many ups and downs, ending in frustrations and failures. They have found that though they are Christians they still have strife in their homes, discord in their hearts, and hunger for everything but the ways of God. They know what they ought to be, but can't achieve it; they are discouraged and cast down. This, I believe, is because so many of us have never learned the secret of walking in the Spirit.

The Bible describes three kinds of people in this world. These are enumerated in the Bible as the natural man, the carnal man, and the spiritual man. Of these, "the natural man" refers to a non-Christian while "the carnal man" and "the spiritual man" refer to two different types of Christians.

The natural man is man as he was born into this world: man born of the flesh, man as he is by human nature. Some people are almost nature worshipers, but they fail to understand that God's creation has been corrupted, and so they are venerating a fallen idol. They do not realize that we are part of a degenerate race whose hearts, the Bible says, are at enmity with God; whose hearts, the Word of God says, are "desperately evil." Man is spiritually dead in his sin and he does not understand the things of the Spirit of God.

If you are not a Christian, you will be absolutely incapable of understanding what I am about to say unless there is a gracious act on the part of the Holy Spirit of God to enlighten your mind. "The natural man receiveth not the things of the Spirit of God, for they are foolishness unto him; neither can he know them." They cannot possibly be known by him unless God reveals them to him. The natural man's horizon is limited to this world. His understanding is limited to human insights. He is a mole groveling in dirt, busily engaged in creating little enterprises, not knowing that they are simply molehills to be stomped into nothing by eternity.

The worldly-wise man supposes himself to be exceedingly wise and clever. He has made all possible provision for himself and has worked out all the angles — but he has made one tragic and fatal mistake: he has left God out of his reckoning. In the end his life will become a tragedy, as deep and dark a tragedy as can be woven from the warp and woof of death and judgment and hell. The self-centered natural man is a "dumb brute beast made to be taken and destroyed," says the Scripture. His affections and aspirations are totally bound by the things of this world. He has forgotten that he is but the creature of the Creator.

If you are in this category of mankind, I warn you that you have no hope beyond this world. You had better enjoy life now, for "it is appointed unto men once to die, and after this the judgment." In that hour, as you stand before the Judge of all the earth, you will realize the truthfulness of the words of Jesus Christ, who said to just such a man, "Thou fool, this night thy soul shall be required of thee: then whose shall those things be?" You must come to realize the folly of your life, the sin of your heart, the extent of your alienation from God, your hopelessness in the judgment, and the worthlessness of your own righteousness. You must come to see that God has provided only one way to heaven, and that this way is through the Lord Jesus Christ. "No man cometh unto the Father, but by me," said Christ. You must come to see that Christ died for your sins and that in him alone is there any hope. You must invite Jesus Christ to come into your heart.

You must also humble yourself. This will be difficult because we are all proud by nature. We have turned pride into a virtue, even though God calls it the chief of all vices. You must by faith embrace Jesus Christ as your Savior and put your trust totally in him. You will become a Christian by receiving Jesus Christ into your heart by faith, thereby becoming a new creature. Christ says of you that you must be born a second time, from above by the Spirit of God. Then and only then will you have any real spiritual and eternal life abiding in you.

If you have been born of the Spirit of God you are a Christian. But there are many Christians who fall far short of the fullness of the Christian life. They find that they still have much of the "old man." They realize that they now have two natures, the old and the new, which are at enmity. They find that they cannot do what they should, so they need to learn to "walk in the Spirit." In order to walk in the Spirit, a person must first be filled with the Spirit of God. God commands us to be filled with the Spirit of God. "Be ye getting filled" is the present continuous tense in the Greek text, and it means the repetitive filling of the Spirit of God — for we are leaky vessels.

How are we going to be filled with the Spirit of God? By first of all yielding ourselves in complete surrender to the mastery of Jesus Christ over our hearts and lives. Many people hold out on God here, or they continue in this or that sin, supposing that this will not affect their lives. They do not realize that this prevents them from being filled with the Spirit of God and the fruit he can bring into their lives.

Second, we must ask the Holy Spirit to fill us. If we are Christians, the Holy Spirit is in us. We are not asking him to come *in* but we are asking him who is in us to completely *fill* us and completely control our lives.

Third, by faith we must believe that he has done this. The Christian receives Christ by faith and believes the promise that he has eternal life. The Christian receives the fullness of the Spirit by asking for it and believes God's promise that he will "give unto us the Spirit" (Luke 11:13) if we will ask him in repentance and faith. Those who go around looking for some ecstatic emotion are denying the very essence of the rule of faith. They deny the promise of God and refuse to believe God's Word. Only as we are filled with the Spirit can we bring forth the fruit of the Spirit in the Christian life.

The Bible says that the Christian should bring forth in his life love, joy, peace, longsuffering, gentleness, goodness, faith, meekness, and temperance. Many Christians, as well as non-Christians, try to do this by their own efforts. This is as futile as a person taking a dead branch, tying on green leaves, and fastening fruit on here and there, supposing himself to have a tree. The first requisite is that there be life in the tree. And so the first thing that is necessary for us is that we be grafted into Jesus Christ by faith. He is the Vine, he says, and we are the branches. We must be grafted into him so that the life-giving power of his Spirit can flow into our lives and produce the fruit of the Spirit.

The works of the flesh, in contrast, are adultery, witchcraft, drunkenness, and other degenerating indulgences. Christ said that those who do these things shall not inherit the kingdom of God. The graces produced by the fruit of the Spirit are his, not the product of our human nature. We have good works which we must do, but the fruits of the Spirit are produced organically by the Spirit of God working in us. This is why all the efforts of an unsaved person to produce virtuous deeds through education, discipline, training, culture, and good intentions are doomed to failure.

This is not to imply that Christians are to ignore the cultivation of moral qualities, because the branch that has been grafted into the Vine must still be pruned and protected from "insects" and "vermin" and "birds of the air." *But the Christian's primary concern must be for the inner life of the branch,* the continual flow of the Spirit of God in his life. Only when this is assured will cultivation and discipline of outward graces be fruitful.

Many Christians spend their days and nights, in effect, plucking bugs from the branches and leaves of their lives, spraying with insecticide, and shielding against wintry blasts, yet their vigor declines and their deeds shrink from lack of sufficient Water of heaven, the Spirit of God, filling and flowing through them. Little water, little fruit.

And how do we walk in the Spirit? "The water that I shall give him shall be in him a well of water springing up into ever-lasting life," said Christ. By asking and confessing and believing, we are filled with the Spirit of God, but by sin we become sieve-like vessels which allow the fullness of the Spirit to diminish and the fruit of the Spirit to wither. Chaos and discord enter our lives. Fighting and arguing begin. Unclean thoughts, covetous-ness, pride, and all sorts of things grow up as weeds in place of the fruit of the Spirit.

We need to learn not only to *be* filled but to be refilled. We do this by becoming sensitive to the work of the Spirit within, and by confessing sin as soon as it appears. Satan immediately accuses: "There, you've blown it! Now what use can God pos-sibly have for you? Just forget the whole thing and come all the way down with me." But God's Word teaches us to confess our sins and to ask again to be filled with the Spirit of God. This is the secret of walking in the Spirit — living by the power and purity of the Spirit.

Bill Bright of Campus Crusade uses the illustration of "spirit-ual breathing": as we breathe out, we confess to God the sin and impurities in our life, and as we breathe in we receive again the fullness of the Spirit of God. Another illustration is that of an automobile. Christ has come into our life, and when we turn over the control to him, he sits in the driver's seat behind the wheel. We, the passenger, have the old nature which wants to grab the wheel and turn into some side path of sin. It happens so quickly — through judgment of others, impatience, anger, envy, deceitful-ness, covetousness, or lust. We must learn to recognize when we are taking over the control of our life from the Lord and surrender again to his direction in the path that is best for us.

Oh, that God would enable us to live in the Spirit! Oh, that we would bring forth the fruits of the Spirit in our lives! Wouldn't it be marvelous to enjoy these fruits in your home and heart this week? One of the fruits of the Spirit is love; what home would not be blessed by the addition of more love and more joy? What would a song do in your home? Another fruit of the Spirit is peace. And there are gentleness, longsuffering, kindness, and goodness — the type of goodness which makes one as saintly in the home as in the church.

I read of a young lady who was walking by Niagara Falls with a group of other people. Her father stopped as they looked at the falls and said, "Let's step aside into this forested place and give thanks to God for the glories of this tremendous sight." Afterward his teen-age daughter said to her friends, "Isn't my father good! But the only ones who know how good he really is are those who live with him at home!"

Are there any of the Spirit's fruits which you would not like to have? Do you want God to bring forth the fruits of the Spirit in your life today? Then yield yourself to the control of Christ and welcome the fullness of the Spirit. His plan for your life is perfect; any other plan will bring you sorrow and loss.

Prepared to Conquer

One of the great tragedies of our time is that so many Americans are totally unfamiliar with the greatest book ever written, the Holy Scriptures. They are also unfamiliar with one of the greatest religious classics ever written, a book which has sold in the hundreds of millions of copies and in every major language of the earth — that grand allegory of the Christian life called *Pilgrim's Progress*. In this marvelous message from John Bunyan's heart we see Pilgrim making his grand tour from the City of Destruction to the Celestial City by way of that hill which has three crosses. The scenes are unforgettable: the Slough of Despond, the dungeon of the castle of Giant Despair, the Delectable Mountain, Vanity Fair, and so on. And how about those characters that so jauntily move across its pages? There are Faithful, Obstinate, Mr. Worldly Wiseman, Mr. Pliable, Mr. Hate Good, and many others.

Pilgrim's Progress is a wonderful book about the most important journey in all the world — the journey from earth to heaven. In this journey Pilgrim comes to a very desolate stretch of road where black clouds block the sun with the darkness of midnight. On either side of the path are great caverns and pits. He trembles as he starts to leave the protection of the hills and walk across this forbidding road. He is not even halfway across when suddenly in his path appears that archfiend, Apollyon, his black wings outstretched, his fangs bared — Satan himself incarnated. With a roar he leaps upon poor Pilgrim. They roll in the road, locked in mortal struggle. Not only life and death but Heaven and Hell are at stake. Pilgrim almost despairs of life itself as his sword is knocked from his hand — the sword of the Spirit, the Word of God. But with one final valiant effort he reaches out and grasps his sword again, and with the power of all-prayer he deals his adversary a mighty blow that sends him scurrying away with a terrible wound.

I will never forget the first time I read *Pilgrim's Progress* and came to those curious words which Bunyan has hyphenated for added effect: "the power of all-prayer." I would like to discuss this often-ignored and little-understood subject.

The Apostle Paul tells us in Ephesians 6 that we are to put on the whole armor of God. He describes the various parts of this weaponry. It consists of wrapping our loins with truth, wearing the breastplate of righteousness, putting the preparation of the gospel on our feet, donning the helmet of salvation, grasping the sword of the Spirit and finally praying with "all-prayer."

Some have thought that this all-prayer is part of the armor of the Christian. However, I think the text indicates otherwise; no piece of armor described would correspond closely to "all-prayer." Rather, we are to take not only the armor of God but also the God of the armor. Even though fully equipped with the armor of God — however complete our protection, however sharp our sword — we are not yet ready to venture into the battle until we call on the General to lead us forth. Without his presence, all of our armor will simply be added weight to bear us down, and prayer is the request that calls forth the General.

When are we to use this power of all-prayer? Says the Apostle, "Praying *always* with all-prayer." These words have a very foreign sound in our modern technological society, for most people not only fail to pray always but fail to pray at any time! Millions of Americans today never lift their eyes to Heaven for help. Some may speak a prayer in a dire emergency, when the knife is at their throats. Others will utter a routine prayer on irregular occasions. But each of these is far from praying always with all-prayer.

Some people are astonished to find that the Bible tells us to pray always. It says this in many ways: "Pray without ceasing . . . in everything give thanks." For every blessing, for every tragedy, for everything that comes we are to give thanks, if we are Christ's, because we know that it comes from a Father's hand and that he is turning it all to our good. He is using it to mold us into the likeness of Christ.

We are to pray in the morning especially. "Early in the morning will my prayer rise to thee . . . my voice thou shalt hear in the morning," says the psalmist. I tremble to think of beginning a day without beginning with God, of undertaking the work assigned to me without the help of the Almighty.

Some people would call this weakness — and they would be right! I am indeed weak, and poor, and needy. "Cursed is the man that trusteth in the arm of the flesh," says the Scripture. Some people feel they are not weak, but they are only displaying their ignorance. For what is man? His life is but a vapor that rises up and vanishes away. As the flowers or grass of the field, it springs up and then is cut down and withers. This is our life. It is a mere handbreadth in God's sight. Those who "lean upon the flesh" are fools indeed. Yet of all the follies of man, perhaps the greatest is his pride. He is so weak that a single microbe can slay him, a single bolt from the blue can rid the earth of any evidence that he ever existed! In a universe so vast that he cannot even see to its extremity, he prides himself that he is something, not knowing that he is but the dust of the ground molded by the fingers of God.

Yes, man is weak. But God can make the weak strong. He can cause to "rise up with wings like eagles" those who wait on him in prayer. "In the morning, in the night, during the day, at the bench, in the office, in the automobile, with the hands in the sink, my prayer shall rise to thee," should be our motto. How important it is that we should pray without ceasing.

But what kind of prayer? "Praying always with all prayer and supplication." The term translated "all prayer" means all kinds and manners of prayer. Paul has told us to put on the whole armor of God. The trouble with many Christians is that they have put on only part of the armor and have been wounded often as a result. They think they have put on the breastplate of righteousness, yet if their closet could speak it would speak of unuttered prayers. Others suppose themselves to have shod their feet with the preparation of the gospel, yet there is unrighteousness in their hearts. Others glory in their knowledge of the Scripture, yet they have never really taken the helmet of salvation. Others have taken that helmet and learned the Word and shod their feet, yet the armor continues to rust day by day, being unoiled by all-prayer. And so the battle is confused. The preparation leads to little or nothing because we go forth only partially prepared and meagerly equipped. "Put on the whole armor of God," says the Scripture.

Even as there are Christians who take only part of the armor of God, who come to the armory of the Lord as to a cafeteria, taking what suits their fancy, so also there are Christians who bend their knees in prayer but leave unsaid much that the Word instructs us to include. The Bible teaches us that there are many kinds of prayers.

First, there is the ejaculatory prayer, that type of prayer which is hurtled heavenward as a speedy telegram in an emergency of life. This is good. There should go up from us hourly such requests for immediate aid, such alarms which awaken Heaven to a need below. For example, you hear the wailing of a siren and the flashing of lights, and the ambulance draws near, then disappears around the corner. Does a prayer shoot forth from your heart to Heaven for this person in obvious need? Or must this sufferer pass by thousands of people who claim to be Christians, yet never look Heavenward in prayer? You see a person by the roadside in trouble. Do you stop? If you do not stop, do you at least breathe a prayer for aid to your Heavenly Father?

We should meet every temptation with prayer. We should enjoy every proper amusement with prayer. We should meet every obstacle with prayer. We should meet every person with prayer, so that the Spirit of God would bring forth such fruit in our hearts that the love and joy and peace of Christ would become obvious to them. We should receive every setback with prayer. We should endeavor in every task to succeed by prayer.

Then there is another type of prayer: the continual prayer, the prayer without ceasing. It is that constant communion between the individual and his precious Savior. Isn't it wonderful that our Lord is not too busy for us! Throughout the day, wherever we may be, we can be in communion with him — a communion that will enrich our lives and bless our hearts and reach out to those around us as well. It is a communion of thankful prayer that can utterly transform our lives. The prayer of thanksgiving can instantly dispel all of those little irritations, those little annoyances, those little disturbances, those little disappointments and grievances in our life, when suddenly we realize how much we have to be thankful for, and how good and gracious our Lord has been to us!

We should mention, too, the closeted prayer, that time of prayer when we get down on our knees alone with the Lord. It should be scheduled every day, for unless it is scheduled it will not come to pass. One of the great battles of the Christian life is to maintain the closet time, that quiet time with the Lord alone when everything else is set aside. Many people are quite willing to pray if they can be doing something else at the same time. Someone told me recently that he often prayed when he was shaving or driving in his car. But one of the real tests of our faith is our willingness to set apart time to pray with the Lord when we have other things to do.

Martin Luther normally prayed two hours each day. However, when he faced an exceptionally busy day he increased his prayer time to three hours in order to obtain extra help from God! When you have a world to change you had better not try to do it on your own!

Then there is concerted prayer, or group prayer. Every now and then I meet a babe in Christ who has read two books in the Bible and comes to the conclusion that prayer meetings are wrong because Jesus said to go into the closet and pray! I just smile, pat him on the head, and know that eventually he is going to read further and find out that it was the custom of the people of God to join together in prayer. God has a special promise for two or three gathered together in his name: If we can agree on anything on this earth, God will hear us. The saints of God from time immemorial have met together in the middle of the week to recharge their spiritual batteries and to pray together, to support one another in their communion with God.

How are we to pray? We are to pray in the Spirit of God. This means that we must realize that Jesus Christ has come into our hearts by his Spirit and that he will help us to pray. ". . . the Spirit maketh intercession for us with groanings which cannot be uttered." We are to pray with the knowledge that the Holy Spirit will edit our prayers and present them perfectly unto God. We are to pray surrendered to Christ, with our lives open to the full control of the Spirit of God. If we are cherishing sins in our lives, God will not hear our prayers. The Scripture says that husbands need to get right with their wives so their prayers will not be hindered.

Finally, we are to pray with all perseverance. Many people have prayed much better at one time in their lives than they do now. Perseverance is needed to continue in what we once did well. Said Paul to the Galatians, "You did begin well. What did hinder you?" Persevere in all-prayer.

What should we pray for? Paul says, ". . . with all perseverance and supplication for all saints." Does the Bible teach that we are supposed to pray to saints? No. The Bible teaches that we are supposed to pray for the saints on earth. Every Christian who truly knows Christ is a saint and yet stands in need of prayer. Do we pray for one another? Do we hold others up by name, praying for them faithfully, remembering their specific needs?

How should we pray for the saints? The Apostle Paul, while a prisoner in Rome, could have said, "Pray that I might be released from these bonds in order that I might speak for Christ." But this is not what he asked! Rather, Paul remained a prisoner in that dark, cold dungeon carved out of stone with one little hole at the top. He had not seen the light of day for two years. He was chained to a Roman soldier, his wrists chafed by the biting iron. Does he pray that he might be released? Does he pray that his temporal and physical condition might be improved? No! Listen to Paul: "Pray . . . with all perseverance and supplication for all saints; and for me, that utterance may be given unto me, that I may open my mouth boldly, to make known the mystery of the gospel, for which I am an ambassador in bonds." He prayed only that his mouth might be opened boldly to proclaim the gospel of Christ! This is to be one of our prayers for the saints.

How sad when this prayer is neglected. For when the oil of the armor is neglected and the God of the armor is ignored, the defenses deteriorate. It is like an island where every harbor is blockaded, or the city of Jerusalem when Titus and Vespasian surrounded it with their armies. They didn't have to go in and cross swords with the Jews. They just sat outside and waited and watched while the city slowly ate itself to starvation. The gaunt, horrible visage of famine spread over the city until finally some were boiling and eating their own children! Likewise, when our harbors and gates of life are closed to prayer, decay sets in and every virtue and grace is gradually consumed.

There is a river whose streams make glad the city of God. It is the river of prayer which carries our petitions to the throne of God and carries back upon that stream vessels laden with the riches of our King. Are you doing business on that stream?

Let me close with an illustration that is meaningful to me. In that precious booklet *My Heart, Christ's Home* is the story of a man who had invited Christ to come and live in the home of his heart. He told of the various rooms. There was one room in particular at the foot of the stairs where he and Christ had made a commitment to meet at the beginning of each day. And it was a wonderful time! The fragrance of that time followed him all day long and made every day a blessing. His heart rejoiced with the experience of it. Then one day something happened. He got up late and had to get to work. He rushed down the stairs and forgot his commitment. The next day he forgot again. After that it was easier. Before long, weeks had gone by and then months. He had forgotten all about that appointed time in the room downstairs. One day as he was rushing past the door he happened to glance into the room, then stopped cold. He backed up and walked into the room. There was Christ. "Lord!" he said, "What are you doing here?" Jesus said, "Have you forgotten our covenant to meet here each morning?" "Yes, Lord, I had forgotten all about it. But you . . . you haven't . . . surely all of these months you haven't been waiting for me every morning!"

"Yes," replied his Lord, "every morning."

Have you remembered your appointment with your Savior? It is the place of victory.

"Merry Tifton to You"

Jesus, the Master Teacher, told parables about things familiar to his hearers. Most of these stories were taken from the rural, agricultural community in which they lived: the sower who went forth to sow . . . the kernel of mustard seed . . . the birds of the air . . . the lilies of the field . . . the shepherd and the lost sheep. From these he wove those enchanting parables which have so grasped the hearts and minds of men.

Most people in America today know little about a sower and sowing, so when I was thinking about preparing a modern parable of Christmas, I decided it should be something related to the television screen! A recent survey shows that Americans spend about forty hours every week watching television!

Do you remember a television program called "The Millionaire"? A fantastically wealthy and unbelievably generous benefactor had the odd habit of giving away a million dollars to various people. His representative was a little man named Michael Anthony, who walked into selected homes, opened his briefcase, and handed the residents a cashier's check for a million dollars! All of this produced some very interesting results. This will be the backdrop for my modern parable of Christmas.

Once in a faraway land, a long time ago, lived a man by the name of John Beersforth Tifton. He was fantastically wealthy, beyond the wildest dreams of avarice. But he had the strange habit of donating a million dollars to certain individuals of his choice. Another gentleman named Michael Anthony would travel to the objects of his generosity and personally give them the money. First there were dozens, then hundreds, and finally thousands all over the world who had become the recipients of his beneficence and thus they had the circumstances of their lives drastically altered.

At his death Mr. Tifton had in the vast holdings of his estate a will which instructed that his generous practices should be continued. Thus it went on for decades, then centuries. Eventually people got together and thought that something ought to be done to remember, to commemorate, to celebrate the memory of this great man. They decided they would commemorate his birthday (which came in the middle of the winter) by having a party and discussing Mr. Tifton and singing songs about him because of his remarkable generosity.

Of course, the only people who were interested in doing this were the people who had been the recipients of the gift — the million dollars. So these millionaires got together in the middle of the winter and celebrated Tifton Day. They wrote poems about him and sang songs. It was a wonderful occasion. Eventually the custom spread throughout the whole world, wherever there were people who had received the gift — the million dollars.

But then something very peculiar happened. Some party-crashing Americans decided to join the festivities. In the midst of the crowd, however, they remained unnoticed. They didn't know exactly what was going on, but it seemed like fun. It seemed to be some sort of celebration about somebody who had made somebody else very rich. This seemed like a nice thing, so they took a glass of champagne and entered into the celebration. They told their friends about it, and the next year they had their own party. In a few years the whole country was celebrating Tifton Day. It was just the right thing to break up the monotony of the long, dreary winter. Soon Tifton Day became a national holiday.

The department stores, with their keen perception, liked this new holiday. Since Tifton Day had something to do with giving things away, they told people it would be nice to give presents to each other — sort of in the spirit of Tifton. So they had "Tifton Specials" and the people bought their gifts. This continued for many years.

One day two gentlemen from that small, faraway land where Mr. Tifton had lived appeared in New York City. It was the day before Tifton. They were hoping they might meet someone who, like themselves, had received Mr. Tifton's million dollars. (Some other Tifton, because Mr. Tifton also adopted the people into his family and gave them his family name.) They hoped they would find two or three people to celebrate the memory of their benefactor with them.

As they walked down Fifth Avenue they looked into a store window. "Only one day left till Tifton!" In the next window, "Tifton Specials, one-half off!" They thought, "My goodness! The owner of the store must be a Tifton! We must go in and meet him. He has certainly used his million dollars well. He has bought a department store!" But just as they started to enter the store, they heard someone shout from across the street, "Merry Tifton!" They turned around and started to go that way. But someone on their own side of the street called out, "Merry Tifton to you!" Before they knew it, all around them was a great chorus of voices shouting, "Merry Tifton and a Happy New Year!" They were utterly, totally amazed! What was going on? Mr. Tifton had certainly been stupendously generous in the number of gifts he had bestowed in America! It was beyond anything they had seen before!

That evening they ended up in a large home in which Tifton Eve was being celebrated. The living room was filled with Tifton cards. (People sent them to their friends every year. They had pictures of snow and animals and said, "Season's Greetings.") A lavishly decorated Tifton tree rose from the floor to the ceiling. Strangely, the visitors could not recall that Mr. Tifton had ever been especially fond of trees. In fact, this type of tree didn't even grow in the country where he had lived! These Americans were certainly strange people! But they did know how to have fun, for

88

many of the guests were totally drunk! The visitors were completely baffled.

Finally one of the visitors said to his companion, "On the street in New York this afternoon did you notice the appearance of the people who were saying Merry Tifton? Some of them were virtually in rags! They didn't look like millionaires at all to me!"

His companion agreed, "Nor did they to me. I can't understand what's going on here."

So they decided to ask another guest. They beckoned to a man nearby and asked him, "Tell me, brother, when did you become a millionaire?"

"How's that?"

"When did you receive your million dollars from Mr. Tifton?"

"A million dollars? I don't know what you're talking about, Mister. I had to borrow $300 from the finance company to buy my Tifton gifts this year!"

"Why are you celebrating Tifton Day?"

"Why am I celebrating Tifton Day? What's wrong with you? Everybody is celebrating Tifton Day! My mother and father celebrated Tifton Day, and so did my grandfather. I've always celebrated Tifton Day! I used to hang up my Tifton stocking on the mantel when I was a child. I thought you foreigners knew all about Tifton Day."

So they asked another man, "Excuse me, sir. Have you received a million dollars from Mr. Tifton?"

"A million what?"

"A million dollars."

"No!"

"Well, could you tell us why you are celebrating Tifton Day? What is this all about? We don't understand it."

"Really? Well, let me see if I can remember. It all started with this man from some foreign country. We think his name was Tifton, but nobody knows for sure. Actually nobody knows whether he ever really lived. Anyway, there's this legend that he used to give away presents all the time — ties, pajamas, handkerchiefs — that type of thing. Somehow we picked up the custom here in America, and so now we give gifts every Tifton Day. After you get used to it you'll get into the spirit of it too."

One of the visitors replied, "Yes, I see what you mean. That sure is a beautiful orange tie you're wearing. I can see this day really does mean a lot to you."

Finally they asked a third man if he had received a million dollars. But he did not know what they meant either. They asked him what Tifton Day meant. He said, "Well, I'll tell you. Mr. Tifton was a very fine man who lived a long time ago. He was very wealthy. We have his biography — it's in a black book. Many of us have it in our homes but I must say we don't read it much. It tells how he made his fortune, I believe. The idea is that if we follow those principles, we can earn a million dollars ourselves, or something like that, I think."

Suddenly, barely audible over the laughter and the tinkling of glasses, came a knock at the door across the room. No one seemed to hear. After a long pause, the door opened, and there stood the perennial descendent of Michael Anthony, briefcase in hand. He had come with a million dollars for someone. "Excuse me . . . excuse me" he began. But no one seemed to be listening. "Excuse me . . ." he began again, but the laughter was so loud that no one seemed to hear him. Finally he turned and left, while the celebration continued hilariously.

That is my parable of Christmas. I wonder if you get cut fingers and sore hands each year from erecting and decorating your Christmas tree. I wonder if you have ever received the *true gift* of Christmas. I wonder if your hands get weary from signing Christmas cards and your tongues satiated with the taste of glue. Do you know what Christmas is all about?

"The gift of God is eternal life through Jesus Christ our Lord." Have you received this gift? Surely this is an infinitely more precious gift than any other we could receive. If you have received this gift you have the greatest riches in the world. You can say with Paul the Apostle, "Thanks be unto God for His Unspeakable Gift."

I wonder how many Americans oh-h and ah-h over ties and handkerchiefs, dolls, toys, dresses, and perfume at Christmas —

while their empty hearts cry out to God for eternal life. I wonder how many will answer the gentle knock of him who says, "I stand at the door and knock; if any man hear my voice, I will come in to him." He is what Christmas and joy and wealth and life is all about! And he wants to come in if you've never made him your Savior and Lord.

Singing at Midnight

The dark night of the soul is something which all of us must pass through. The deep valley, the great darkness awaits everyone on this dying earth. The suffering of my own wife motivates the presentation of this message. As we search the Scriptures, we find three basic attitudes which men take toward our inevitable afflictions.

The most common reaction to suffering is described by Elihu in the book of Job. "But none saith, Where is God my maker, who giveth songs in the night" (Job 35:10). In oppression, many cry out to Heaven, but their cries are as the cries of a wounded animal raising its howl into the wind. Elihu concludes that the oppressed are little better than the oppressor because both are crying rebelliously against God. No one seems to be asking in his affliction, *"Where is God my maker?"* Instead, everyone cries out, *"Why? Why me? What have I done to deserve this?"* They fling their reproaches against the brassy heavens — the cry of a wounded animal. "There are so many others who deserve it more than I do. After all my service! If this is your God you can keep him!" As one woman said to me, "Explain this to me and then I'll buy your religion." But my religion is not for sale, nor do I believe that she could have comprehended the explanation.

Then there are those who are like the mariners carrying Paul captive to Rome. That great twenty-seventh chapter of the Book of Acts describes the awesome storm at sea when Euroclydon, the great tempest, overtook their ship. Day after day, night after night, they saw neither stars nor sun. They were driven head on with the wind, not knowing where they went. As they took soundings for depth, they found that they would soon smash against the rocks. That would mean the end. And so they cast four anchors from the stern and waited in grim resolution for the morning. Now this is a somewhat more noble attitude to take in times of night . . . to wish for the morning . . . to hold on . . . to square your jaw. It is what the British mean by keeping a stiff upper lip.

But this is not what the Bible would have us to do. Why do we not call: *"Where is God my maker, who giveth songs in the night?"* God is a magnificent Director; his most precious songs are sung in the night. Of all the songs of all the songbirds, none equals the beauty that comes when inky blackness covers the earth, when the moon is hidden and darkness shrouds the night — and from that darkness comes the song of the nightingale, singing out its heart in the blackness of night! *"God my maker, who giveth songs in the night"* — that is our text.

It is easy, said Charles Spurgeon, to sing in the daytime. Most birds do it, and many men do it too. It is easy to sing when our cup is brimming full, when wealth swells in abundance and health is ours, when all things are going well and success crowns our every effort. Yes, it is easy to sing in the daytime. But what about the night, when life crumbles in and all our hopes are dashed? Then the song chokes in the throat. The singing stops and the gloom of night sets in. It is easy for the aeolian harp to give its sweet music when the soft winds blow, but what about that dead stillness of soul that comes when hope has flown? Now where comes the fullness of music? It is easy to make a crown when jewels are scattered at our feet. But when there is nothing but hard stones, of what shall we make our diadem?

Songs in the night . . . a paradox? *Songs! Night!* They do not seem to go together! Yet God would have us to know that they *do.* The great Apostle Paul, the greatest of Christians, said in Philippians: "I have learned in whatsoever state I am, therewith to be content." Spurgeon points out that Paul said, "I have learned," for this is not something that comes naturally to human beings. Often the school is difficult and the lessons try us to our depths. Weeds grow quickly. We do not need to cultivate thorns and thistles and brambles. We do not need to teach men how to grumble and gripe and complain and murmur, for these weeds flourish in the fallen nature of man. But if we would have precious flowers, the luxurious garden, we must have the tender care of the gardener. We must learn at his feet. Therefore, he says, let us be patient students in the college of contentment. This is the great lesson we must learn.

Were these the idle words of a preacher, without meaning or substance? Look at Paul's life! Look at him that night in Philippi! In the very city to which he wrote these words he had given eloquent proof of their reality. He was dragged before the magistrates . . . hissed at and howled against . . . beaten with a whip until his back was a bloody pulp . . . cast into stocks . . . placed in the innermost cell of the prison, unable even to recline upon the floor. And now the long night hours begin. Suddenly the darkness is shattered by the sound of singing, and Paul and Silas sing praises unto God — at midnight! In the very depths of the darkness of that night, their voices brought forth songs unto God, and the results were tremendous. The shackles fell off. The doors were thrown open. For a person who can sing in a situation like this, there can be no prisons, and iron bars can never hold his spirit. For his soul is free; his spirit is at liberty. He has learned the great secret of changing circumstances into sanctuaries and rejoicing in the Lord his God.

Is he alone? Are there any others? Have you read the magnificent song of Habakkuk in the Old Testament? The lyrics should be known by all and engraved upon our hearts: "Although the fig tree shall not blossom, nor fruit be in the vines; the labor of the olive shall fail, and the fields shall yield no meat; the flock shall be cut off from the fold, and there shall be no herd in the stalls: Yet I will rejoice in the Lord, I will joy in the God of my salvation."

Songs in the night . . . these are songs which catch the ear of the world more than any other. But whence do they come? Where do they arise? Our text says, "God my maker, who giveth songs in the night." They cannot be wrung out of the human heart that is broken. They are a gift of God. God gives songs in the night.

I think perhaps the most difficult task I have ever faced was that of breaking the unexpected news of cancer to my wife. I looked at her on her bed, knowing that she expected to rise and go home in just a few minutes. "It's benign, isn't it?" she asked. "No, Dear, I'm afraid it's cancer." Never have I experienced such knifelike words. I felt like Abraham — as though I had driven that knife into her heart. But that knife was driven into my own heart as well. It plunged deep into my soul. As I walked those halls that day, with no one to talk to, there was one thought that kept coming back to my mind. It was the words of Lincoln in the depths of the war, after the death of his son, when he said to Henry Ward Beecher, "I think that I shall never be glad again." On that day I did not see how I could ever be glad again. It did not seem to me that I could ever stand in the pulpit again to lead in songs of praise. I was plunged into the dark night of the soul.

But God gives songs in the night. Only shortly thereafter, while riding in my car, the words of the Doxology burst spontaneously from my lips: "Praise God, from whom all blessings flow; Praise him, all creatures here below"; and the Gloria Patri: "Glory be to the Father, and to the Son, and to the Holy Ghost." That is a song that only God can give! The Word stands sure that God does indeed give songs in the night! I shall never forget hearing my wife pray these words: "I thank Thee, Lord, for what has happened to me this summer." These are wonderful songs. They are divinely-given songs, for we are not strong in ourselves.

The world listens with an attentive ear to these songs. A woman across the hall with a broken shoulder, bemoaning her fate, with seemingly no hope when all was dark, was so astonished by the testimony of Anne that she asked Christ to come into her life. The telephone calls that Anne received and her joyous response to the questions was so remarkable that the telephone operator of the hospital called one day and asked to come and see her. And she came . . . and she came again . . . and again. The night before we left she asked Christ to come into her life! These are indeed songs that the world desperately needs to hear.

Someone has paraphrased the words of Christ: "I have a message for thee, my beloved, a message which can turn thy gloom into joy and can illumine thy heart. It is only five words, but let them sink deep into thy soul. It is this: *"This thing is from me."* There it is, my friend. There is the secret: to recognize the hand of a sovereign God in all that comes to us. What is your problem? What is the night of your soul? Is it a financial reverse? "This thing is from me — that you may draw upon my riches." Is it sickness? "This thing is from me — that in your weakness my strength may be made perfect." Do others turn their backs upon you? "This thing is from me — that you might be drawn closer to me."

This world is not ruled by chance. When the dark night settles upon your soul . . . when the night winds like a black stallion beat their hoofs against the shutters of your house . . . when the whining of its voice sounds like the very banshees of hell — may I remind you that firmly in the stirrups, with hands upon the reins, is our Lord. We need not fear. He is in control. "Think it not strange concerning the fiery trial which is to try you, as though some strange thing happened unto you." God is at work. He is taking a piece of human clay and fashioning it into the likeness of God.

This "fiery trial" can be illustrated by the goldsmith of old. The refiner of gold would put the ore into a crucible and light the fire beneath it. As the gold would melt, the imperfections within it would melt also and would rise to the surface. Then with a stick the refiner would skim the impurities away. The fire would burn even hotter, and more imperfections would rise to the surface to be skimmed away. Finally, when the purifier could see the reflection of his face perfectly in the gold of the crucible, his task was finished. "When thou passest through the fires, the flame shall not burn thee; I only design thy dross to consume and thy gold to refine."

God is the Master Sculptor. Will we resist the strokes that will fashion us into his likeness? Or will we rather rejoice as we yield ourselves into his hands! If we know him and realize that his banner over us is love . . . that nothing can come to us except what first passes through the heart of a Father's love . . . that all that comes to us he has promised by that amazing miracle of his love to transform into our good, if we realize this, I repeat, we can look up with joy and sing songs in the night!

One Way

Christian churches across the United States and around the world resound with praise for Jesus Christ. Sermons extol his spotless life, his matchless teaching, his marvelous examples. Yet a question often remains unasked and unanswered that mars or destroys the ministry of Jesus Christ. It is a question that modern Americans do not want to ask — much less to answer. The question is this: Is Jesus Christ the *only* way to God? Granted that Jesus was a great teacher, even the greatest teacher that ever lived . . . that he founded the noblest religion on the face of the earth . . . that his life was without equal, is he the only way to God?

With all the religions of the world which modern man can investigate, is Jesus Christ the only way to God? In a space-age world where Africans build skyscrapers instead of spearing crocodiles, the question haunts us: Is Jesus Christ the only way to God? In a world where people once labeled "pagan" now speak with us through the TV in our living rooms, in a world where men of all religions and no religion preside over Americans and Europeans at the United Nations, the question becomes crucially urgent: Is Jesus Christ the only way to God? Is he the only way to heaven? In a world teeming with exploding humanity we must know whether Jesus of Nazareth is the only true way to God.

Some may grant that he is the *best* way, the *highest* way, the *noblest* way, or even the *shortest* way, but the real question is: Is he the *only* way? Who would be presumptuous enough to answer that question? Would you? Would I? Should the churches collectively presume to answer this question? Can anyone answer this question with finality?

The question is answered by Jesus Christ himself: "I am the way, the truth, and the life: No man cometh unto the Father, but by me." This statement by Christ could hardly be more explicit.

How can we respond to this? In a modern electronic world where Asia is no longer months away, where Africa is no longer the mysterious continent, but where all the peoples of the world become neighbors via Telestar, what shall we say to this statement? Shall we say that Christ was wrong? Shall we say that the text has been misinterpreted? But I have not "interpreted" it at all; I have only quoted what Christ said!

Let us investigate whether Christ was quoted correctly. Maybe the analogy of other Scripture will enlighten us. Let us look. "Neither is there salvation in any other, for there is none other name under heaven, given among men, whereby ye must be saved," said the Apostle Peter to the Jews (Acts 4:12). Jesus expressed this in other ways. He said, "I am the door: if any man enter in, he shall be saved. . . . He that entereth not by the door into the sheepfold, but climbeth up some other way, the same is a thief and a robber."

Someone asks, "What about all these other religions and the good men who founded them?" I repeat Christ's decree: "All that came before me were thieves and robbers." Jesus Christ clearly claims that there is no other way. The Bible repeatedly makes statements such as these: "He that honoreth not the Son honoreth not the Father." Anyone who does not honor Jesus Christ is not honoring God. Anyone who does not have Jesus Christ does not have God.

"What about the people who worship God in other ways?" The Bible says that the heathen do not worship God, but instead worship Satan! These are hard words — hard for me and hard for you. The real question is not whether these words are hard to accept but *whether they are true.* Some of the truest things that have ever been spoken have been agony for some people to accept.

Let's suppose, then, that those statements of Scripture quote Jesus correctly, but they still are not true; what then? We have a mistaken Christ, a deluded Christ, or a deceiving Christ, and therefore not a divine Christ. According to the Bible, Jesus Christ is God and therefore he cannot be wrong. He is either right, or he is not God. If he is wrong, he is merely human and subject to errors and weaknesses like the rest of us. Christianity stands or falls upon the truth of Christ's repeated declaration: "He that believeth on the Son hath everlasting life, and he that believeth not the Son shall not see life, but the wrath of God abideth upon him." This is the word of Christ to every American, to every Jew, to every Muslim, to every Hindu, to every atheist, to every Confucianist.

Christianity stands on the truthfulness of these words. If they are false, the deity of Christ is a myth, the inspiration of the Bible is a mockery, the testimony of the Church for twenty centuries is a lie, and the world missionary movement is wasted heroism. All of these are based on one fact: that the world without Christ is lost, alienated from God, and on its way to eternal hell! This is why Christ came! If this seems difficult to accept because so many people do not know Christ, remember that only a handful knew him when he came! And why did he come? "I came to seek and to save that which was lost." This includes all the people of the world, for "all have sinned and come short of the glory of God."

Why don't people like to hear this? There are several reasons. Some people say, "Oh, God couldn't do that to the heathen!" But what they are really feeling is, "God would not do that to *me.*" This attitude is based on a distorted understanding of Christianity. It assumes that Christianity is essentially similar to all other religions of the world — that it consists primarily of a set of ethics and morals and commandments, and that if a person does the best he can to follow this code and succeeds fairly well, then all will be well. But this is the essence of paganism; it is the very antithesis of Christianity. Christianity does not say that a man will be saved by doing the best he can, living according to commandments, or following a set of rules, but rather that *a man cannot save himself at all* . . . that he is *utterly hopeless* . . . that he is *bound in his sin* . . . and that unless God comes down and dies for him he cannot be redeemed at all! It takes nothing less than the death of the Creator to save the creature, and that is exactly what Christianity is all about!

Christianity is the very opposite of all other religions. Christ is unique in that he claims to be God. Buddha never claimed this; Confucius never claimed it; Mohammed never claimed it; nor do any of the followers of any of the other religions of the world claim this for their founders. But Christ claimed it and proved his claim by rising from the dead. Christ *is* the very God by whom all things were made, according to Colossians 1. The Scripture says that there is nothing that is made that Christ did not personally create. Jesus Christ made Gautama Buddha, he made Zoroaster, he made Lao-tse, he made Confucius, he made Mohammed — he created them! And the Bible says that one day they will be on their knees before him confessing that he is God!

The clear, keen mind of Napoleon saw this very well. He said, "Superficial minds see a resemblance between Christ and the founders of other religions." If you see such a resemblance, you have a superficial mind, according to Napoleon. There is between Christ and the founder of every other religion the distance between the finite and the infinite, between the human and the divine; between man and God. For Christ is God or else he is a fraud. Either Christ is the *only* way to God or he is no way at all. Which is it?

A second reason for disbelieving this truth is that people can thus feel relieved of the responsibility of responding to it. For twenty centuries the Christian Church has based its entire expansion upon Christ's statement that mankind is lost without him. The Apostle Paul, David Brainerd, William Carey, Hudson Taylor, Adoniram Judson, David Livingstone, and countless others have pierced the deepest jungles with the gospel of Jesus

Christ. Why? Because they were convinced that men in their sins were alienated from God and were on their way to judgment, and that they desperately needed a Savior. This is why missionaries have given their lives and spilled their blood on every continent of the world.

Notice that Jesus said, "No man cometh unto the *Father* but by me." Men apart from Christ may come to God as a *Judge.* In fact, they not only *may* but they definitely *will!* That is exactly their problem! They are all going to stand before the Judge of all the universe! When they stand before him it will be as violators of whatever light they had, whether the light of creation displaying the Creator or the light of conscience which every man possesses, or the full illumination of the gospel of Jesus Christ. All men have done things that they know in their hearts to be wrong. They have done them under cover of darkness. They have done them with deceit and lies. They have condemned their neighbors for it, yet they know that they themselves are guilty. And they will be judged accordingly at the great Day of Judgment. By the light of creation they know there is a God, but they have chosen to be idolators, worshiping beasts and men and creeping things. And so they are guilty. God must condemn them.

No man can come to the reconciling, loving, gracious Father except through him who went to a Cross to make it possible. Christ is the way, the truth, and the life — not merely a way, a truth, and a life. *He is the only real truth.* "Show us the Father," said Philip. "He that hath seen me hath seen the Father," said Christ. Truly God has visited this planet.

But how do we respond in America today? Every century has its heresy, and the great heresy of the twentieth century is the heresy of universalism. Many modern Americans are saying, "It's just not necessary. The natives are all right. They'll get along. They've got their gods. After all, if a man is sincere he'll be all right, won't he?" The Bible answers with a resounding "No! You are condemned already because of your sins!" If by any stretch of the imagination man by good works could ever have gotten himself into the presence of God in paradise, then what in the name of heaven was God doing by sending his own Son to die on the Cross? All of this talk drives a dagger into the very heart of Christianity.

If you say you believe that all men will get to heaven some day, and that eventually "all roads lead to Rome," don't call yourself a Christian, for you have just called Christ a liar! You have stripped him of his deity, robbed him of his sovereignty, and made him into a mortal like yourself! Jesus said, "No man cometh unto the Father but by me!"

We don't like the responsibility of knowing that a world is perishing. We would prefer to close our eyes and bury our heads in the sand. We don't want to become involved in the burden of reaching a lost world. We don't want to share the burden of Christ, who looked down from the Mount of Olives at Jerusalem and wept, saying, "O Jerusalem, Jerusalem . . . how often would I have gathered thy children together, even as a hen gathereth her chickens under her wings, and ye would not!" We do not want to weep with Jesus.

We do not want to weep over Jerusalem and we do not want to weep over America. We would rather by a simple snap of our fingers take everybody to paradise. We have not said with the Apostle Paul, "I say the truth; I lie not, the Spirit of God bearing witness with my conscience that I have a continual burden and heaviness of heart for my kinsmen according to the flesh. I could wish myself accursed from Jesus Christ for their sake." Paul anointed his pillow with tears for lost men — because they were *lost.* Can we do less — and be ready to meet our Lord?

"Go ye into all the world, and preach the gospel to every creature . . ." for, "I am the way, the truth, and the life; no man cometh unto the Father but by me!"